THE
BEST
OF
UNIVERSAL

THE
BEST
OF
UNIVERSAL

BY

TONY
THOMAS

The Vestal Press, Ltd.
Vestal, New York 13851-0097

ACKNOWLEDGMENTS

——⚬∞⚬——

My primary source of research in studying the history and the films of Universal has been the library of the Academy of Motion Picture Arts and Sciences in Los Angeles, and I am grateful to Linda Mehr and her staff. In illustrating the book, my thanks in full measure go to Frank Rodriguez and Corinne de Luca of the Stills Department at Universal. I am particularly grateful to Nancy Cushing-Jones in the realization of this book.

Library of Congress Cataloging-in-Publication Data
Thomas, Tony, 1927-
   The best of Universal.

   Includes index.
    1. Universal City Studios — History.
  2. Motion pictures — United States — History.
  I. Title.
PN1999.U57T47 1990   384'.8'0973   90-12824
ISBN 978-0-9115-7292-6

Printed in the United States of America.

First printing 1990

CONTENTS

———∞———

Universal begins with the purchase of the 230-acre Taylor Ranch in Lankershim township at the east end of the San Fernando Valley in June, 1914. Within a few months, the first administration building appeared, fronting on what is now Lankershim Boulevard. This view is directly west, down the completely rural valley.

Sixty years later, not only is the lot covered with acres of buildings and sound stages, but the entire San Fernando Valley, twenty miles long and ten miles wide, is packed with houses and stores, crisscrossed with thousands of streets, and home to a population of more than a million.

In 1930, looking eastward across the Universal backlot of a small and prosperous little motion picture company. At the upper left stretches the city of Burbank with Warner Bros. studios at its western edge and Disney Studios behind.

In 1990, Universal is the biggest film operation in Hollywood with most of its acreage covered with office buildings, sound stages, hotels and restaurants, backlots, parking lots, and visitor facilities that mark it as one of America's most popular tourist attractions.

THE MAGIC KEY

He looked a little like a genial gnome and he stood a shade over five feet in height, but he casts a long shadow through the pages of Hollywood history. Carl Laemmle was the enterprising German immigrant who founded Universal Studios in New York in 1912 and, three years later, bought a large tract of land in California to set up the world's first film studio — complete with a backlot and all of the facilities needed for the production of movies. When he opened the gates on March 15, 1915, Laemmle let it be known that "This is Universal City!" It still is today.

Carl Laemmle's foresight, drive, and energy forged the company in those chaotic, early years of Hollywood into a viable, progressive business. He was one of that handful of pioneers who invented an entirely new industry; in view of all else that has gone on in the world since 1915, it is hardly surprising that the studio Laemmle founded has had its ups and downs. Any entertainment complex able to endure and prosper over a long period of time does so only because of constant change, adaptation, and development. Public taste has never been an easy graph to cipher. But Universal has good reason to be proud. It has survived for more years than any other studio, and it is now by far the biggest, most active, and most productive entertainment center in the world.

The Magic Key

Carl Laemmle got into the picture business when he opened his own theater in Chicago in 1906. Within a year, he not only owned several other theaters, but he had set up a film rental service, getting his movies directly from the producers and renting them to other theater owners. Laemmle was already on his way to becoming a movie mogul. By 1909, he had his own production company with the grand title of "Independent Moving Picture Company of America," which quickly became known as IMP. IMP was a good name for a company owned by a happy, feisty, little fellow like Laemmle, who might have been referred to as a leprechaun had he been Irish instead of German.

IMP's first picture was a one-reeler — about twelve minutes — called *Hiawatha* and filmed in the "wild west" of New Jersey. Like many Europeans, Laemmle had a fascination with the American West. That fascination has had great bearing upon the course of American film. Instinctively, he knew that people wanted to see other people in action, preferably outdoors. California was obviously the promised land for the moviemaker. It not only had all kinds of scenery, but it had a balmy climate that allowed for filming all year round. Laemmle was not alone in thinking that it would be easier to try making pictures there than in New York and New Jersey. But he was the only one of those early moguls with the savvy and vision to take such a major gamble on the future.

Carl Laemmle — about to become Hollywood's first movie mogul. Lankershim Township presents him with a key of solid gold with which to open his gates . . .

In early 1914, Carl Laemmle bought the 230-acre Taylor Ranch in the east end of the San Fernando Valley just over the Cahuenga Pass from Hollywood. He paid $165,000 for it, and the consensus was that he had stuck his neck out on a doubtful venture. Within a few years, the consensus changed. Laemmle's Universal City became the first

. . . and with the turn of that key, Universal City, the first community ever built for the sole purpose of making films, begins its history.

Thousands of people descended on Universal City that day, walking, eating, sitting around, and generally being entertained by the movie folk.

municipality designed as a town rather than just a studio built for the purpose of making movies. He had advanced the picture business in one giant step by bringing the factory concept to it.

Laemmle knew something else about picture making that had not quite dawned upon the other moguls: the value of publicity. For his opening day, which spilled over into the following day, Laemmle invited thousands of guests. He entertained them royally. They watched movies being made — especially Westerns with cowboys and Indians galloping all over the place. But what these delighted people were actually seeing was the birth of Hollywood as the major center of American film making. It was the start of Universal City, but it was also the start of a great deal more — a new, exciting, rapidly developing industry that would have an incalculable impact on the world.

Laemmle ran his Universal City with a firm hand for twenty years. His policy was as simple as it was successful: family entertainment. He was right in believing that his tastes were just about those of the average man. He liked Westerns, comedies, and melodramas. But more importantly, he had a sense of programming. He felt that moviegoers would

enjoy more than just the main feature, so he had his company set up units for making newsreels, shorts, cartoons, and serials.

Time, of course, eventually caught up with Carl Laemmle. He was 69 years old when he retired in 1936; he died three years later.

There have been a number of managements since Laemmle's time, but the studio's policy has remained constant: entertain the public with movies that touch upon every phase of human life. And not simply amuse them, but occasionally inspire them, always bearing in mind the enormous power and potential of film.

Universal City today is a vast entertainment complex involved not only with the production of movies for the theater and television, but with a variety of allied enterprises, not the least of which is the Universal Studios Tour, now one of the world's major tourist attractions. Visitors enjoy the exciting atmosphere of moviemaking, and those who are true movie buffs delight in knowing that these Universal hills are alive with memories, with countless images and talents. It all began when Carl Laemmle, beaming with enthusiasm and optimism, turned that magic key.

Much of the entertainment comes in the form of Wild West shows, signalling what would soon be a Universal specialty — the making of movies about cowboys and Indians.

Hollywood's first Western street would soon expand into facsimiles of all kinds of streets depicting all parts of the world. In the next fifty years, Universal would rarely shoot film anywhere outside of these couple of hundred acres.

CLASSIC UNIVERSAL

Nobody sets out to make a bad movie. They are all designed to be good and successful. Movies are made with care and enormous expenditures of talent, time, money, skill, and hope. And those are just a few of the ingredients.

But if nobody sets out to make a bad movie, neither does anybody set out to make a classic. That is a dimension of moviemaking that cannot be designed. It is that certain something, a touch of magic that gives a film an identity all of its own. It goes beyond working with a fine script, excellent actors, and a gifted director — plus all of the splendid craftsmen who supply music, photography, sets, and costumes.

The classic film is the one in which all of the elements blend in such an unaccountably marvelous manner that it is immediately an individual entity. More importantly, it is a film that never loses its identity; the passage of time gives it even more identity. That kind of film is a classic. Universal has had its share of them, and its first classic films came about through the talents of one of the most incredible actors in the history of Hollywood: Lon Chaney.

Lon Chaney began his movie career as an extra in 1912 after a dozen years in the theater, and he quickly established himself as an actor capable of assuming almost any identity. Chaney had a genius for make-up and physical contortion. His ability to assume grotesque guises reached the classic level in 1923 when he appeared as the poignant and pitiful Quasimodo in *The Hunchback of Notre Dame*. Producer Irving Thalberg, then 24 years old and known as "The Boy Wonder of Universal," backed Chaney with extensive sets, including a replica of the great cathedral of Paris. The results are still looked upon as a master piece of cinema.

Lon Chaney was a major figure in the Silent Era. He was dubbed "The Man with a Thousand Faces." In 1957, Universal paid tribute to his contributions by making a film with that title and giving the role of Chaney to James Cagney, himself one of the most distinct and powerful talents in Hollywood lore. Cagney underwent many of the difficult and physically taxing Chaney guises, including a re-creation of the 1923 filming of *The Hunchback of Notre Dame*.

In 1923, the few residents of the San Fernando Valley are surprised to find this superb replica of Notre Dame Cathedral nestling in the Lankershim Hills. It is built for the Lon Chaney production of *The Hunchback of Notre Dame*.

Chaney's next Universal classic was *The Phantom of the Opera* in 1925. Again he blended the grotesque with the poignant in portraying a pitifully disfigured musician who lives in the cavernous sewers beneath the Paris Opera House and menaces the House in revenge for his injuries. The only tender spot in his heart is for a lovely young singer (Mary Philbin); sadly, his appearance only serves to terrify her.

For Chaney's *The Phantom of the Opera*, Universal built its largest sound stage to accommodate a re-creation of the Paris Opera House complete with a 100-foot-wide stage. Much of the set, on Stage 28, still stands and remains for the visitor to view as one of the few remaining bits of evidence of the great Silent Era of picture making.

The set was used again in 1943 when Universal re-made *The Phantom of the Opera* with the esteemed Claude Rains as the tormented musician and soprano Susannah Foster as the reluctant object of his affections. The handsome Technicolor remake offers generous helpings of opera sung by Foster and Nelson Eddy, and a performance from Rains that is both touching and frightening. Rains preferred to wear a rubber mask rather than risk comparison with Chaney's make-up genius. The result is no less impressive.

(Above) Chaney's version of Quasimodo is re-created in 1957 by James Cagney for *Man of a Thousand Faces*. Universal's tribute to the actor who had done so much for them in their early years.

(Below) *Man of a Thousand Faces* also pays tribute to the young producer who made *The Hunchback of Notre Dame* for Universal — Irving Thalberg, played by Robert Evans.

Lon Chaney is also the star of *The Phantom of the Opera* in 1925, together with a scared Mary Philbin.

In 1943, *The Phantom of the Opera* is remade with Claude Rains as the musician who becomes hideously disfigured and takes to the sewers. Here, he tries to strangle music publisher Miles Mander as Gladys Blake gets ready to throw the acid.

Other stars of *The Phantom of the Opera*: Nelson Eddy, Susannah Foster, and Edgar Barrier.

Several wars have come and gone since Universal made *All Quiet on the Western Front* in 1930, but no film has surpassed this one in depicting the waste and misery of the battlefield. Considered an industry risk because it tells its story from the German side of the lines, it became an immediate success with critics and public alike, winning the Oscar as Best Film of the Year.

The studio built a small German town on the backlot and re-created the World War I frontlines on location at a ranch fifty miles from Hollywood. With acres of trenches, barbed wire, mud, and shell craters, director Lewis Milestone held moviegoers spellbound with his scenes of men advancing, retreating, and being cut down by the thousands with machine gun bullets and shells. Shrapnel, bullets, and bayonets take their meaningless toll of young men of all nationalities; and all illusions about the glory of war soon vanish. Milestone's starkly realistic scenes of battle are made even more effective by his skillful direction of the group of youngsters who go straight from high school to the Western Front and find themselves immersed in horrors that they could never have imagined.

Chief among them is a quiet, dignified boy — Lew Ayers in a performance that made him an instant star — who discovers the true horror of war when he bayonets a French soldier in a crater and then, because of the shelling going on around him, has to remain in the crater watching the man slowly die. Time has done nothing to diminish the message nor the magnificence of *All Quiet on the Western Front*.

For *All Quiet on the Western Front* in 1930, Universal builds a German town in which to parade soldiers on their way to the trenches . . .

. . . trenches so realistic that they look like the real thing.

In 1930, Moss Hart and George S. Kaufman mercilessly satirized Hollywood in their Broadway comedy *Once in a Lifetime.* Two years later, Carl Laemmle amazed Hollywood by buying the play for the screen. The general felling was that Moss and Kaufman had cut a little too close to the bone in poking fun at the more lunatic fringes of Hollywood life, but Laemmle felt that it was time the industry had a laugh at its own expense. He was right. *Once in a Lifetime* was not only one of Universal's biggest hits in 1932, but much of its humor is still on target.

Gregory Ratoff plays Herman Glogauer, the dictatorial head of a movie studio (a man barely on speaking terms with sanity), and Jack Oakie is the minor-league vaudevillian who is mistakenly hired as head of production and whose every ludicrous error somehow becomes construed as a stroke of genius.

But *All Quiet on the Western Front* is really about the short military life of young Paul Baumer, played by Lew Ayres, pictured here with Ben Alexander.

Once in a Lifetime: Jack Oakie, Sidney Fox, Gregory Ratoff, Aline MacMahon, and Russell Hopton.

Back Street: John Boles and Irene Dunne.

The so-called "woman's picture" was an important commodity in Hollywood's Golden Age. In terms of material content, these carefully tailored movies were the forerunners of today's television soap operas.

One of the most basic and durable movies in this category is Universal's production of the Fannie Hurst novel *Back Street* in 1932. It made a star of the beautiful Irene Dunne as she played the role of a young lady who, by accident, misses out on marrying the upperclass gentleman (John Boles) whom she loves. When they meet six years later, he is married and the father of two children; however, she still loves him and agrees to become his mistress, comfortably set up in and apartment on some New York back

street. Within these limitations, they lead a fairly happy life — until his death and the realization that it will be his widow and not his mistress who will attend his funeral.

Admits the sorrowful mistress: "There's not one woman in a million who has found happiness in the back streets of a man's life." The critics may not have derived much enjoyment from *Back Street,* but the public most certainly did.

In 1941, the studio gave *Back Street* another handsome treatment starring Charles Boyer and Margaret Sullivan. It was made one more time in 1961 with Susan Hayward and John Gavin.

The *Back Street* of 1941 with Charles Boyer, Frank McHugh, and Margaret Sullivan.

The *Back Street* of 1961: John Gavin and Susan Hayward.

Imitation of Life (1934) with Rochelle Hudson and Claudette Colbert.

In 1934, novelist Fannie Hurst provided Universal with a winner in the "woman's picture" category with *Imitation of Life*. Claudette Colbert portrays a young widow with a baby who goes into business with her black maid. Both ladies become wealthy but not happy; they each have daughters who cause problems. Colbert's daughter (Rochelle Hudson) falls in love with the man (Warren William) whom mother wants to marry. The daughter of the black woman can pass for white and stirs up racial tensions — a heavy theme for 1934, but one that helped this expertly crafted soap opera find a huge audience.

Imitation of Life appeared again in 1959; this time as a vehicle for one of Hollywood's most famous and glamorous stars: Lana Turner. The racial themes are even more dramatic, but the main emotional focal point is the triangle caused by lovely Sandra Dee as the daughter setting her sights on handsome John Gavin, the man her mother hopes to marry. The remake proved to be even more effective, thanks to the sumptuous production values given it by producer Ross Hunter.

Imitation of Life (1959): John Gavin and Lana Turner.

In 1935, Irene Dunne starred in another movie aimed squarely at female moviegoers: *The Magnificent Obsession*, an extremely popular treatment of Lloyd Douglas' extremely popular novel. In this film, Irene plays the widow of a distinguished doctor whose death is partly attributed to the irresponsible actions of a handsome young playboy (Robert Taylor) who is also a medical student. She angrily rejects his romantic advances and on one occasion, runs from his presence and becomes involved in a traffic accident. Her injuries include being blinded. At this, the young man resolves to change his flippant lifestyle and devote himself to his studies.

A few years later, he has become not only a respected surgeon, but a Nobel Prize winner. Without letting her know his identity, he operates on the widow and restores her sight. Eventually, she comes to realize that he has become the same kind of gifted, dedicated man whom her husband was, and she responds to his love.

As improbable as *The Magnificent Obsession* may seem in a brief summary of its plot, the film had no problem pleasing and seeming plausible to audiences all over the world. It proved just as effective when the studio remade it in 1954 with Jane Wyman. Just as the original version had helped make a star of young Robert Taylor, so did the remake fix young Rock Hudson firmly in the affections of masses of admirers. With *The Magnificent Obsession*, Rock's career shifted into high gear.

Irene Dunne in *The Magnificent Obsession* (1935).

The 1954 version of *The Magnificent Obsession* starring Rock Hudson and Jane Wyman.

When 34-year old Carole Lombard died in a plane crash while engaged in a war bond drive in 1942, Hollywood lost a unique lady. She was that rare blend: an elegantly beautiful woman with a gift for comedy. In 1936, she co-starred with William Powell in *My Man Godfrey*, a comedy with a sting in its tail. It satirized the Great Depression by contrasting the plight of the unemployed with the apparent disdain of the wealthy. And it took the skill and charm of players like Lombard and Powell to make the unlikely premise amusing.

The man of the title is a Bostonian aristocrat reduced to poverty and capriciously dragged out of a hobo camp to serve as a "forgotten man" at a Park Avenue party. He expresses his disgust to his hosts, but it serves to win him a job as their butler. At this, he proves expert. It also wins him the love of the family's delightfully wacky daughter. Much as he tries to resist her, she finally has her way; no man could be luckier.

The years have not robbed *My Man Godfrey* of any of its wit and charm, and it serves to remind us how fortunate Hollywood was to have once enjoyed the presence of the delectable Carole Lombard.

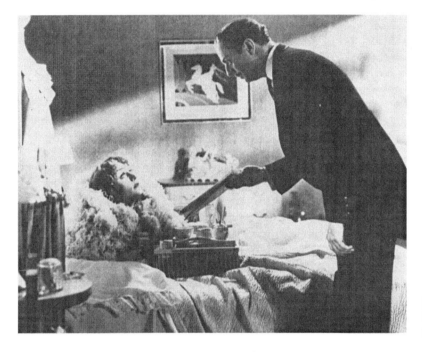

In 1936, the delightful Carole Lombard falls in love with *My Man Godfrey* in the form of William Powell.

And in 1957, it is June Allyson falling for the Godfrey of David Niven.

The best way to describe *Flash Gordon* is to say it was the *Star Trek* of its day, not simply because it dealt with adventures in future space, but because it inspired the same wildly devoted following. Universal decided to film the comic strip in 1936 as a thirteen-chapter serial, each running about twenty minutes; a budget was set of $350,000 — three times the usual amount allocated for a serial. It quickly became the most successful serial ever made, resulting in two sequels: *Flash Gordon's Trip to Mars* (1938) and *Flash Gordon Conquers the Universe* (1940).

Larry "Buster" Crabbe, who came to Hollywood's attention through his triumphs as an Olympic swimmer, proved to be the perfect choice as the American space hero who defeats the attempts of the evil Ming (Charles Middleton), Emperor of Mongo, to become dictator of the universe. Helping him is his lovely girlfriend, Dale (Jean Rogers), and Dr. Zarkov (Frank Shannon), the brilliant scientist who created the rocketship in which Flash and his party traverse the skies. The adventures of Flash Gordon kept millions of young fans in a state of excitement on Saturday afternoons in the late 1930's and made its producers feel very happy.

There was always talk around Universal of doing *Flash Gordon* as a feature film. It finally happened in 1980 with Sam J. Jones as the stalwart space warrior and the distinguished Swedish actor Max von Sydow as the merciless Ming — plus the kind of technical wizardry and special effects about which the original production team in 1936 could only have dreamed.

Buster Crabbe as *Flash Gordon*, adventuring through space with Jean Rogers as Dale Arden.

In the lavish and sumptuous remake of *Flash Gordon* in 1980, the hero is played by Sam J. Jones with Ornella Muti as Princess Aura.

Sherlock Holmes and the Voice of Terror (1942), the first of the twelve Universal films with Basil Rathbone as the master sleuth, always aided by the wonderfully befuddled efforts of Nigel Bruce as Dr. Watson.

Sherlock Holmes — Basil Rathbone. It is doubtful if the movies have ever struck upon a better bit of casting than this. The lean, serious image of Rathbone with his precise English diction seems exactly the kind of man whom Sir Arthur Conan Doyle had invented for his tales of crime and detection. Almost as exact is the choice of Nigel Bruce for Holmes' close friend and associate, Dr. Watson. The Bruce version of Dr. Watson, genial and somewhat bumbling, is the perfect foil for the intellectual, infallible Holmes of Rathbone.

The two actors were prominent members of Hollywood's then flourishing British colony, and many others from that colony were employed in the making of the Holmes movies.

In mid-1942, Universal contracted Rathbone and Watson to do a series, the first of which was *Sherlock Holmes and the Voice of Terror*. An immediate hit, it led to eleven other films in the series, ending with *Dressed to Kill* in 1946. They were all made as secondary features; yet, they have outlived most of the main features they were meant to accompany. Universal's twelve Holmes adventures are perpetually shown on television and are now sold on video cassettes as well.

When Rathbone finished with the series, he was so identified with Holmes that he decided to leave Hollywood and resume his stage career in order to break the image. Eight years passed before Rathbone returned to the movies, and he never again appeared on screen as the master sleuth. But he could never break the image: Sherlock Holmes — Basil Rathbone.

The last of the twelve films: *Dressed to Kill* with Mary Gordon, who supports Rathbone and Bruce in every outing as their kindly landlady, Mrs. Hudson.

The Rex Beach novel *The Spoilers* had been made into films three times previously by other studios, but Universal comes up with the master version in 1942 with Randolph Scott, Marlene Dietrich, and John Wayne.

The Spoilers, the famous Rex Beach novel about gold mining in turn-of-the-century Alaska, was first filmed in 1914, then in 1923, and again in 1930. Twelve years later, Universal decided to do another rendition, one that turned out to be the definitive version.

Marlene Dietrich was hired to play the owner of a glittering saloon in Nome, and John Wayne and Randolph Scott were brought in as her co-stars. The choice could hardly have been better. Wayne is the adventurous young gold miner, and Scott is the gold commissioner with a streak of larceny. Both of them vie for Marlene's love, although there is little doubt that the winner will be the honest miner. Aside from giving a flavorful acount of those exciting, but dangerous, gold fever-ridden days in Alaska, *The Spoilers* is noted for the fist fight between Wayne and Scott, a true classic of well-choreographed, extended bar room brawling that has never been equalled.

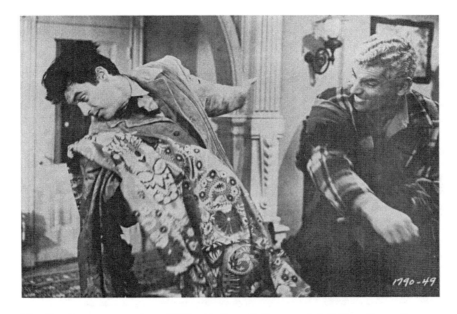

The Spoilers was remade in 1955 with Rory Calhoun and Jeff Chandler as the battling heroes.

Hollywood greatly benefitted from the migration of talent from Europe in the Nazi-dominated years of the 1930's. Among these immigrants was Fritz Lang, perhaps the foremost director of the German cinema. Lang had a darkly dramatic style; he was at his best when depicting humans trapped in dire situations. *Scarlet Street* (1945) is a fine example.

The story is that of a drab little man (Edward G. Robinson) married to a harridan who scoffs at his hopes of becoming a painter. His romantic fantasies find expression in his paintings until he falls in love with a beautiful, but scheming girl (Joan Bennett) who takes advantage of him and has him set up in an apartment. To do this, he resorts to stealing money and becomes a slave to the girl. This is acceptable to him until he discovers that she and her boyfriend are manipulating him to get more money as well as stealing and selling his paintings. He goes beserk and kills the girl with an icepick. Circumstantial evidence points to the boyfriend, who goes to the electric chair, leaving the drab little man to spend the rest of his days brooding over his guilt.

Scarlet Street is classic Fritz Lang: tragic, romantic, and poignant as well as being a fine reminder of a brilliant character actor, Edward G. Robinson, whose more than eighty films unfailingly brought public and critical acclaim. Strangely, not one of them resulted in his being nominated for an Academy Award. Incredibly, Robinson was a star Oscar actor overlooked.

Scarlet Street with Edward G. Robinson and Joan Bennett.

Alfred Hitchcock spent a considerable portion of his Hollywood years at Universal, beginning with his 1942 wartime espionage thriller *Saboteur* and concluding with his black-humored mystery *Family Plot* in 1976. Hitchcock was one of the few directors whose name really had impact at the box office, and he was the only director who became a "Personality" in his own right. His droll manner, drawling English accent, and wickedly cherubic appearance elevated him to stardom when he hosted his television programs in the years 1955 to 1962. Almost all Hitchcock movies deserve citing as classics, but there were two films he made at Universal that defy any other classification.

Shadow of a Doubt (1943) was a film that Hitchock himself particularly liked. He claimed it brought murder and violence "back into the home, where it rightfully belonged." It is a perfect example of this wily director's style, the core of which is setting up macabre vibrations in seemingly calm and commonplace surroundings. In this case, Hitchcock insisted on filming his story in an actual small town — a revolutionary consideration in Hollywood in those years. He chose Santa Rosa, California, and picked Thornton Wilder of *Our Town* fame as one of his scenarists to give the picture as much folksy Americana as possible.

The doubts that shadow the story are cast by the visit of a genial gentleman (Joseph Cotten) to his relatives in Santa Rosa. He and his niece (Teresa Wright) become good friends; but after a while, she begins to sense something strange about him. It turns out that he is a murderer, having disposed of three wives for their money. The niece fears this knowledge will cause her own death; but circumstances put an end to her uncle before this can

Alfred Hitchcock begins his long association with Universal in 1942 with *Saboteur*, starring Robert Cummings and Priscilla Lane.

Shadow of Doubt with Charles Bates, Henry Travers, Edna May Wonacott, Teresa Wright, and Joseph Cotten.

Tippi Hedren being menaced by one of *The Birds*.

The Birds would not dare menace the master, Alfred Hitchcock.

happen, although not before the audience has been manipulated by Hitchcock's fiendish cat-and-mouse technique in the art of suspense.

The Hitchcock book of tricks was also devilishly apparent when he made *The Birds* in 1963. Again, he chose to film his story in a small California town — this time in Bodega Bay, a fishing community north of San Francisco. In this strange excursion into chilling fantasy, the villains are not humans but birds — not feared birds of prey but masses of sparrows, hawks, and seagulls that, for no apparent reason, take it into their heads to attack and murderously ravage the inhabitants of the community. It is the very ordinariness of the birds, as Hitchcock

well knew, that makes their actions so terrifying. They peck certain people to death; they attack houses so ferociously that they smash through windows and down chimneys; and eventually, they cause a fire in the town. Then, after several days of siege, it is all over — the birds quietly sit back on fences and telephone lines as the humans anxiously move away. Was it a matter of our feathered friends expressing their contempt for humanity? The capricious Sir Alfred never bothered to explain; he simply enjoyed himself as his audiences squirmed and squealed, helping him rack up another great success in his conspicuously successful career as a master movie maker.

The last of the Hitchcock films for Universal: *Family Plot* with Barbara Harris and Bruce Dern.

Burt Lancaster became an instant front-rank movie star with his performance in *The Killers* in 1946. While multitudes of young men try desperately to break into Hollywood, Lancaster simply walked in on the basis of having appeared in only one play on Broadway. His physique and mystique made him a natural film actor.

The Killers, masterfuly directed by Robert Siodmak, is an imaginative expansion of a short story by Ernest Hemingway telling of a boxer named Swede who has been marked for murder by crooks. Hemingway's story is an exercise in fatalism and gives no reason why the man must die. The skillful screenplay by Anthony Veiller uses the original material at the beginning of the film and then flashes back to the circumstances that might have produced the situation. In Veiller's view, the boxer is a man who has allowed himself to be taken over by racketeers; and through the cunning of a beautiful, but deceitful girl (Ava Gardner), his life has become a mess. In finally defying the crooks, he realizes that he is signing his own death warrant, but he stoically waits for the killers to come and get him.

The key to the success of *The Killers* is the poignant performance of Lancaster as the tough, but vulnerable Swede; however, he is abetted by every facet of film craftsmanship.

The Killers, starring Burt Lancaster, Jeff Corey, Albert Dekker, and Charles D. Brown.

Ronald Colman won a richly deserved Oscar in 1948 for his performance in *A Double Life*, the story of a distinguished but demented Broadway actor, that is skillfully scripted by Garson Kanin and Ruth Gordon, and subtly directed by George Cukor. Since all of these people had considerable knowledge of the theater, they were experts in supplying all of the right touches.

Colman's handsome, but increasingly insane, matinee idol is a man far more dangerous than his colleagues realize. He finds it harder and harder to differentiate between his own psyche and those of the characters he plays, especially Shakespeare's own Othello. Finally, his mind breaks; in the scene in which Othello kills Desdemona, the actress (Signe Hasso) does, indeed, die.

A Double Life was a *tour de force* for Ronald Colman and the high point in his career. He appeared in three other films in the remaining ten years of his life, but he must have known that he would never be able to top his performance in this magnificent movie about the theater.

A Double Life: Signe Hasso and Ronald Colman.

Orson Welles as the repugnant lawman Hank Quinlan in *Touch of Evil*.

In less-inspired hands, *Touch of Evil* (1958) might have been just another crime picture; but with Orson Welles' subtle, moody directions and his portrait of a fat, sweaty, malevolent, and corrupt policeman, it was destined to become a prime item in the *film noir* category. Welles wrote the screenplay, adapting it from the novel *Badge of Evil* by Whit Masterson.

The story is set in a small American town on the Mexican border with part of the action taking place on the other side of the line. Hank Quinlan (Welles) is not only Chief of Police, but apparently the chief of everything. He is obsessed with bringing criminals to justice and not above manufacturing evidence or manipulating the law to his own gain until he sinks in a morass of his own making. Welles' playing of Quinlan makes him just about the most repugnant policeman *ever* portrayed on the screen. There is something nightmarish, evil, and fascinating about Hank Quinlan and his world. Welles guides his audience on a nervous, compelling trip into that bizarre, brutal world. One of its inhabitants is Quinlan's mistress and the keeper of a brothel, played with dark, low-keyed sensuality by the incomparable Marlene Dietrich.

Of all the massive movies dealing with ancient history, *Spartacus* (1961) is by far the most intelligent. The credit belongs to Kirk Douglas, who not only played the title role but also served as the film's executive producer. Indeed, he was the driving force behind the film. It was his decision to hire Dalton Trumbo to write the screenplay and the then 32-year-old Stanley Kubrick to direct it.

Spartacus was a Thracian slave who led a band of rebels in an escape from the gladitorial school at Capua, 130 miles south of Rome, in 73 B.C. After two years of revolt, Spartacus headed an army of 90,000 men that beat the Romans in every battle except its last when the rebels were hopelessly outnumbered and in which Spartacus lost his life. But his spirit lived on; through the centuries, he has become a symbol for all revolutionaries.

Spartacus contains no chariot races and no orgies, but it does convey the grandeur and the decay of ancient Rome. It also contains one of the most impressive battles ever staged on film. Douglas took his company to Spain for the exteriors and employed 8,000 soldiers of the Spanish Army to perform in the battle when the Romans devastate the rebel forces. Apart from its obvious pictorial values, *Spartacus* is an especially well-cast picture. Kirk Douglas gathered an impressive group of actors including Peter Ustinov, whose performance won him an Oscar. In the scene in which Douglas battles the magnificent Woody Strode, he is watched by Jean Simmons, Nina Foch, Laurence Olivier, John Dall, and Joanna Barnes. By any yardstick, *Spartacus* is a classic.

Spartacus: the slaves' revolt is led by Kirk Douglas, John Ireland, and other angry gladiators.

The less ferocious side of *Spartacus*: Jean Simmons and Kirk Douglas.

To Kill a Mockingbird with Mary Badham and Gregory Peck.

Harper Lee won a Pulitzer Prize for her novel *To Kill a Mockingbird;* when her book was made into a film in 1963, her choice of actor for the leading role of lawyer Atticus Finch was Gregory Peck. Indeed, it seemed as inevitable as Clark Gable playing Rhett Butler.

To Kill a Mockingbird is a beautiful evocation of a place and time — a small town in the South in the early 1930's — and it strikes a happy balance between sentiment and reality. Atticus Finch, a widower, makes a modest living and does his best to bring up his young son and daughter by himself. One of his problems is guiding them in a community fraught with racial strife, especially when he takes on the case of a young black man (Brock Peters) accused of rape. He believes the man to be innocent and makes a dignified and plausible defence, but to no avail. The trial is the dramatic highpoint of *To Kill a Mockingbird,* although it is not the real substance of the story, which is a recollection of the childhood and memory of a wonderful father — a man dedicated to justice and truth. Gregory Peck was the personification of the role, and it surprised nobody when it earned him an Oscar.

Veteran producer Hal B. Wallis brought Maxwell Anderson's play *Anne of a Thousand Days* to the screen in 1969 and wisely cast Richard Burton as King Henry VIII and Genevieve Bujold as his second wife, Anne Boleyn, whom he executed after those thousand days as his Queen. Both actors brought the necessary fire and spirit into their roles, making the film a battle of the sexes amid the panoply of history. Filmed in England and using actual locations, it provided audiences with a vivid lesson in the bloody politics of 16th century England; but as producer Wallis well knew in making the picture, no matter how magnificent the settings and the costumes, it would be the performances of his stars that would make *Anne of a Thousand Days* a classic film. Burton as the fierce-tempered, dictatorial monarch consumed with ambition and passion for his Anne, and Bujold as the courageous young girl who can't help loving him, yet who is not afraid to look him in the eye and tell him that he is a vicious beast are perfectly cast in their roles.

"Nobody has ever talked to me like that before!" bellows the King. It is a rare moment in the annals of movie confrontations.

Anne of a Thousand Days, starring Genevieve Bujold and Richard Burton.

In 1970, producer Ross Hunter, a man with his finger on the pulse of public taste, invested $6,000,000 into turning Arthur Hailey's best-selling novel *Airport* into a *Grand Hotel* of the airways. It was the kind of film that critics enjoy knocking. Be that as it may, it was a box office blockbuster and set the style for the whole genre of movies about disasters.

The concept called for an all-star cast with Burt Lancaster as the pivotal figure — the manager of a huge airport. Plaguing him are a tremendous blizzard, runways blocked with mounds of snow, an airliner stuck on a runway, trade union picketers, airport commissioners worried about inadequate facilities and the complaints of residents in the airport, his neglected wife (Dana Wynter), a lovely airline agent (Jean Seberg) eager to be his mistress, a philandering pilot (Dean Martin) married to the manager's sister (Barbara Hale) but playing around with a stewardess (Jacqueline Bisset), a charming old lady stowaway (Helen Hayes), a demented man (Van Heflin) intent on blowing up a giant passenger jet in flight, and the man's distraught wife (Maureen Stapleton).

Airport is high-grade pulp fiction done with top-grade professionalism. And as an illustration of what it is like to be in a jetliner when a bomb goes off, it is all too real.

Airport: Dean Martin and Burt Lancaster.

The Sting: Paul Newman and Robert Redford.

All films are gambles; but if there is a fascinating story to tell and if Robert Redford and Paul Newman star in it, the odds are more than favorable that it will be a successful gamble. *The Sting* (1973) could hardly fail.

As a pair of charming confidence men in the 1930's, Redford and Newman skillfully set up a racketeer (Robert Shaw) who is responsible for the killing of a friend. Since the racketeer is a cold, humorless man, the audience is tickled by the elaborate scheme in which the chums bilk him out of $500,000 in a cunningly tilted game.

The Sting is a sidetrip into the world of cardsharks, cheats, and rogues. No one would willingly subject himself to being conned by such appealing swindlers as this pair, but it is a treat to watch them work over someone who deserves to be fleeced, especially with the music of Scott Joplin tinkling away in the background. It is no con to claim *The Sting* as the classic con picture or to point out that it won an Oscar as Best Film of 1973.

Summertime packs the sandy shores of Amity Island off the Massachusetts coast with happy vacationers. Also happy are the island businessmen who derive a nice livelihood from catering to the tourists. Into this blissful scene swims a most unwanted intruder — a huge Great White Shark that makes its presence known one moonlit evening by turning a beautiful girl into a meal.

Jaws, of course, is the film that made the whole human race think twice about setting foot into the ocean again; and a film that shaped up into a masterpiece of suspense and dread, thanks to its brilliant young director, Stephen Spielberg. Peter Benchley's best selling novel was well served by Spielberg and his crew, who did all of their location filming in the waterways around Nantucket Island and

Martha's Vineyard, giving the viewer an accurate picture of what happens when a little paradise is struck by fear. The big fish, big in meanness as well as body, finally meets his end when a marine scientist (Richard Dreyfuss), a policeman (Roy Scheider), and a grizzled old shark hunter (Robert Shaw) combine forces — but not until the audience has been wrung dry with emotion and fear.

Jaws was well represented in the 1975 Oscar nominations. One of the coveted gold statuettes went to Verna Fields, whose blending of actual shark footage with shots of the mechanical version of the beast created shock waves; and to John Williams, whose ominously pulsating music is a textbook example of what film scoring is all about.

In *Jaws*, Robert Shaw gets ready to shoot the menacing beast, and Richard Dreyfuss is set to throw over air-tight barrels.

Henry Fonda and Katharine Hepburn in *On Golden Pond*.

The least surprising Oscar ever won by an actor was, happily, the one given to Henry Fonda in the spring of 1982 for *On Golden Pond*. The only surprise involved was that this most respected of American film actors had never before received an Oscar. But even without that factor, Fonda would have won for this poignant study of a man reluctantly observing his 80th birthday while staying at his summer home in the country with his wife of 48 years (Katharine Hepburn). Adding to the poignancy is the visit of his daughter, with whom he has not had a close relationship. The fact that this role was played by Jane Fonda gave the film an extra dimension since it is public knowledge that the actor and his daughter had, themselves, some difficult times over the years.

On Golden Pond also brought Hepburn an Oscar, her fourth, as the compassionate, understanding wife of a man emotionally and physically staggered by the passing of time. The film, therefore, succeeds on two levels: first, as a touching account of aging, produced with taste and intelligence; and second, as a vehicle for two stars whose particular talents will never be seen together again.

Henry Thomas and his friends out to save E. T.

Films to which the word "enchantment" can be applied are precious few, and fewer still if they appeal to adults and children alike. Stephen Spielberg pulled off such a piece of magic with his *E. T. The Extra Terrestrial* (1982), the story of the friendship that grows between a young boy named Elliott (Thomas Henry) and a strange-looking creature from another planet. The creature is lost on Earth when he fails to get back on his spaceship and comes under the protection of Elliott. Seemingly ugly at first encounter, the creature soon reveals a warm and gentle nature — in addition to confusion as he takes his first drink of beer and feels as he has never felt before.

A triumph of special effects, no invented being has ever touched the heart more keenly than E. T. In the end, he must return to his planet. He asks Elliott to come with him, but the boy knows that he cannot. Instead, he asks E. T. to stay, but the kindly creature knows that that is not possible either.

With a musical score by John Williams that lifts the film like a giant unseen hand, Spielberg's actors and artisans create a fantasy full of charm, humor, and kindness; and one in which a weirdly wonderful little creature, an extra-terrestrial, teaches us something about the spirit and the soul of living beings, whether from this planet or another.

With *Sophie's Choice* in 1982, Meryl Streep further proved what had been apparent for a long time: that she is among the most extraordinary actresses *ever seen* in films. In terms of her uncanny ability with accents, she may be the most extraordinary actress of all. *Sophie's Choice* required her to speak English with a Polish accent.

As difficult as that might have been, she achieved even greater facility with a Danish accent for the glorious *Out of Africa,* which won an Oscar as the Best Film of 1986. Produced and directed by Sidney Pollack, it was based on stories Baroness Karen Blixen (who wrote under the name Isak Dinesen) wrote about the years she spent in Africa in the early part of this century. Unhappily married to a philandering Danish aristocrat (Klaus Maria Brandauer), Blixen falls in love with a dashing British sportsman-hunter with the grand name of Denys Finch-Hatton (Robert Redford). Sadly for Karen, the charming and amusing Denys is not a man who believes in marriage. He is later killed in an airplane crash just as Karen is leaving Africa after losing her coffee farm.

But *Out of Africa* is not simply about love. It is a wondrously visual picture about the human spirit and its reaction to a unique region of the world — a place of vast, shimmering landscapes full of meadows, rich vegetation, and mystical mountains, to say nothing of a range of animals of endless fascination. The use of Mozart's beautiful, measured clarinet concerto for the musical score underlines the juxtaposition of British civilization to this land and its native peoples. Pollack's film captures all that can be seen and felt in Dinesen's elegant, perceptive stories; Meryl Streep captures the spirit of that exotic, almost mystical woman.

Out of Africa: Meryl Streep and Robert Redford.

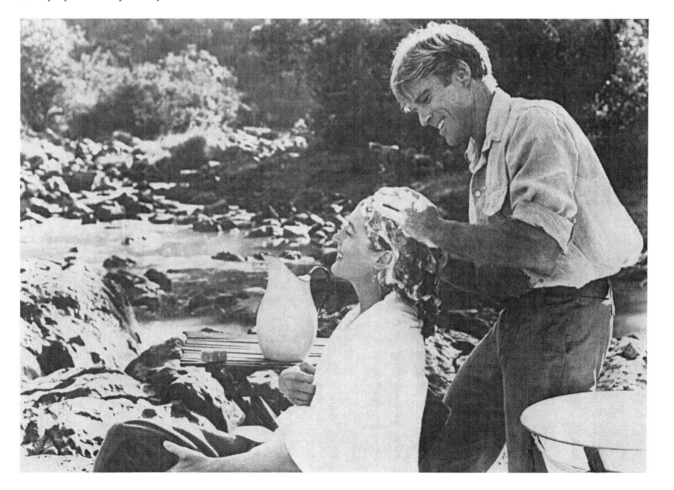

Sigourney Weaver as Dian Fossey in *Gorillas in the Mist*.

All of the dedication and compassion that marked the life of controversial American anthropologist Dian Fossey was brought to the screen in 1988 with a riveting performance by Sigourney Weaver in *Gorillas in the Mist*. Quite apart from the superb photography of the awesome settings in the rain forests of remote African mountains, the film is a character study of a woman whose fascination with gorillas gradually turned into an obsession and, eventually, led to her death. No one has ever discovered who murdered Fossey; it may have been natives who misunderstood her concern for the animals or it may have been the poachers against whom she had spoken out with such strong contempt. All of the complexity, courage, and commitment of this unusual woman is vividly conveyed by Weaver in a performance that is almost as dedicated as Fossey's life to the gorillas.

Filmed over the course of three months in elevations as high as 18,000 feet, spending hundreds of hours with gorillas to capture them on film at their closest and most intimate contact, Weaver deserved all of the praise that later came her way. She conveys Fossey's growing sense of paranoia, one which costs her the love of a photographer (Bryan Brown) who wants her to leave Africa and become his wife. She chooses to stay until attachment to her cause brings her to an isolation from which there is no return. An amazing woman. An amazing performance.

WILD WEST — MADE TO ORDER

The fascination with the American West is — and there is no better word to describe it — universal. Nobody knew that better than Carl Laemmle. He loved Western stories; and when he opened his studio, he built a permanent Western town on the backlot as well as stables and a large bunkhouse for the cowboys whom he hired as extras. For many years thereafter, Universal production teams never needed to go on distant locations to make Westerns; they simply roamed through the hundreds of acres of the North Hollywood hills that comprise the Universal lot to this day.

Laemmle's first Western star was Harry Carey, who appeared in dozens of two-reelers during the Silent Era and later became a well-known character actor in talkies. Carey was the man after whom John Wayne fashioned his own Western image. Wayne was a nine-year-old fan at the time this 1916

The first of Universal's Western stars is Harry Carey, pictured here wearing a plaid shirt on an open sound stage in 1917 as visitors in a stand beside it watch. Universal was the first studio to encourage visitors, who were charged an admission fee of ten cents.

Harry Carey, with crossed arms, plays opposite Olive Gordon, soon to become Mrs. Carey. In later years, both would be among Hollywood's most active character actors.

sequence (see photo) was being shot at Universal. Harry Carey is the central figure in the group at the left; the lady is Olive Gordon, who later became Mrs. Carey. Many years later, she and Harry became stock players in the classic Westerns of director John Ford. And where did John Ford get his start? Shooting Westerns for Carl Laemmle at Universal.

During the 1930's and 1940's, the "B" Western, usually running an average of sixty minutes and made on a very modest budget, was as much a staple of Hollywood productivity as the situation comedy was on television on the early 1980's. This was certainly true at Universal, where the studio contracted series with most of the top Western stars at one time or another. Four of the best of them merit considerable attention: Tom Mix, Ken Maynard, Buck Jones, and Johnny Mack Brown.

Prior to his being signed by a film company in 1911, Tom Mix served with the U. S. Army in the Spanish-American War and was a deputy marshall in Oklahoma as well as a star of the rodeo circuit — all of which made him a natural for the movies. More importantly, he had a flair for publicity and limelight, almost singlehandedly inventing the movie image of the cowboy as a brave, adventurous, colorful character. His antics on and off screen made Mix the highest paid movie star of his day. In 1932, he agreed to make a series of Westerns for Universal and completed nine of them before deciding to retire from the screen. His salary of $10,000 a week was equal to the entire budget of most "B" Westerns, but Carl

Laemmle knew it was worth every penny to finally corral the most flamboyant and legendary Western actor of all.

Tom Mix, the first of Hollywood's cowboy heroes, ended his movie career after making nine Westerns at Universal.

With the retirement of Tom Mix, Universal next enticed Ken Maynard to be its leading Western star. The handsome Maynard had gained fame as a rodeo star, and he is reputed to have been the finest horseman ever to become a film cowboy, doing tricks far beyond the range of the stuntmen who usually double for stars. No one ever accused Maynard of being a good actor, but neither could he be accused of short-changing the millions of Saturday matinée fans who saw his pictures for their exciting action.

Of all the movie Westerners, the one most noted for authority and a true interest in telling good stories

The best of Ken Maynard's Westerns for Universal, *The Strawberry Roan* (1933), with Ruth Hall.

was the dignified Buck Jones. Universal contracted him in 1934 on the understanding that he could set up his own production unit and be in charge of the choice of material. As a result, the twenty-two films he made at the studio set a new standard in the genre. There was a mystique about Buck Jones; when he died a hero's death in 1942, rescuing people in the Cocoanut Grove fire in Boston, he became a legend.

Between 1934 and 1937, Buck Jones is Universal's biggest Western star, making 25 well-crafted movies.

Among the best of the Buck Jones Westerns at Universal: *Smoke Tree Range* with Muriel Evans and Dickie Jones.

Johnny Mack Brown had the longest tenure of any Western star at Universal, beginning in 1937 and ending six years later after doing four serials and 28 features. Brown came to fame in the late 1920's as a star halfback on the University of Alabama's football team. There was always a gentlemanly Southern charm about him, but he was also convincing when swinging a punch and handling a six-gun. His pictures were the high-water mark in Universal's long and honorable association with "B" Westerns.

Johnny Mack Brown makes an appearance in Abbott and Costello's *Ride 'Em Cowboy* (1942) along with Anne Gwynne.

One of the best Westerns of Johnny Mack Brown is *Lone Star Trail* (1942), well-remembered by Western buffs because of its savage barroom brawl between Brown and a young villain named Robert Mitchum.

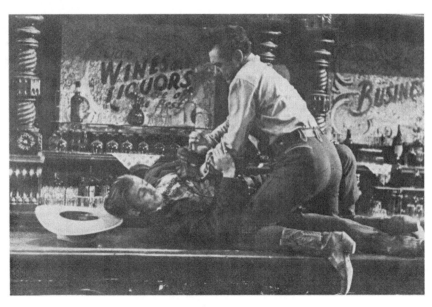

Times were changing. Up until the late 1930's, the Western, with few exceptions, was a "B" picture and aimed especially at weekend showings for millions of small boys all over the world. Hollywood gradually discovered that the fascination with the American West had a far wider market than that. Universal made the discovery in 1940 with its exciting production of *When the Daltons Rode,* relating the adventures of a family that became outlaws when its Kansas farmlands were stolen. The scriptwriters of Hollywood found the 20-year period following the end of the Civil War in 1865 to be particularly rich in incident, and they took a good deal of liberty in making it even more rich.

Every major male star was required to spend at least a portion of his time in the saddle. To Randolph Scott, this requirement was highly agreeable. This gentlemanly actor from Virginia with his quiet strength, soft accent, and dignity seemed to personify the ideal Westerner; gradually, he became a specialist in this kind of film. *When the Daltons Rode* was one of the movies that helped shape Scott's career. It gave him the role of a lawyer who tries to point out the injustice being done to the Daltons and falls in love with one of them (Kay Francis). But as in all good Westerns, it is not the love interest that brings in the customers; it is the marvelous work done by hordes of skillful stuntmen in setting up chases, street fights, barroom brawls, and train robberies. *When the Daltons Rode* did particularly well in the latter department.

Randolph Scott may have been the star of *When the Daltons Rode*, but that is Broderick Crawford throwing the punch.

Destry Rides Again was a vehicle for Tom Mix in 1932 and for Audie Murphy in 1955. But the classic version of this film appeared in 1939 with James Stewart as the mild-mannered, gunless sheriff who cleans up the frontier town of Bottle Neck and Marlene Dietrich as the barroom entertainer who helps him do it. The casting for both roles was perfect. Audiences responded to Stewart's boyishly charming portrayal of a pacifist-with-a-punch, and they were especially delighted with the sultry Dietrich's account of the seemingly tough and worldly lady whose heart has been waiting for the right man to come along. *Destry Rides Again* was a triumph for Marlene, who returns to the characterization that had made her an instant star a decade earlier in *The Blue Angel* — the sensual cabaret singer who drives men mad. Indeed, the same composer who had written the music for that famous movie, Frederick Hollander, was hired to write the songs for *Destry Rides Again*. One of them, "The Boys in the Backroom," turned out to be a Dietrich classic.

Destry Rides Again, starring James Stewart and Marlene Dietrich.

James Stewart was initiated into the celluloid West with *Destry Rides Again* in 1939, playing a gentle, gun-shunning sheriff. A decade passed before he next appeared in Western garb, but this time there was a vast difference in image. When he signed with Universal to make *Winchester '73* in 1950, he was a more mature actor, and the genre of the Western film had itself matured. Now it was more adult and more realistic, and, therefore, more interesting.
In *Winchester '73,* Stewart is a man bent on finding the murderer of his father. He finds him in Dodge City and competes with him in a marksmanship contest. Stewart wins a Winchester rifle, but the murderer steals it and takes off. In the ensuing adventures, the weapon passes through a number of hands before Stewart retrieves it and uses it to despatch his adversary.

Winchester '73: James Stewart and Horace McNally.

Canyon Passage (1946) was Universal's first Western to be filmed on a distant location. The company sent cast and crew to the magnificent Rogue River country of Oregon to tell the story of a pioneer settlement in 1856; they came back with stunning Technicolor footage. Dana Andrews is the hero who saves the community from Indian attacks provoked by a despicable villain (Ward Bond). Here and there throughout the story, that delightful character Hoagy Carmichael wanders in to sing a few songs, including one that turned out to be a classic: "Ole Buttermilk Sky."

Canyon Passage: Susan Hayward and Dana Andrews.

The Far Country with Ruth Roman, Steve Brodie, and James Stewart.

James Stewart and Anthony Mann headed north again in 1954 to make *The Far Country*, a story set in Alaska but filmed in and around Jasper National Park in Alberta, Canada. The Technicolor cameras caught a lush setting for this tale of a cowboy who supplies beef to gold-hungry hordes and runs afoul of rustlers. He finds out just how tough things are in this kind of world.

Winchester '73 was a career advancement for Stewart as it was for his talented director, Anthony Mann. Mann, whose career was cut short by a heart attack in 1967, was responsible for a number of the finest Westerns ever made, several of which starred Stewart. In 1952, they took their talents to Oregon, along with a vast number of actors and technicians, to make *Bend of the River,* which tells the story of early settlers in that state. The story called for a wide range of spectacular scenery, including rich farmlands, forests, and rivers, plus a wide range of activities like gold mining, wagon trains, outlawry, and Indian attacks. *Bend of the River* is no mere Western, but an epic slice of Americana.

Bend of the River, starring Jay C. Flippen, James Stewart, and Rock Hudson.

Cattle Drive with Joel McCrea and Dean Stockwell.

Like Randolph Scott, Joel McCrae began his movie career in the early 1930's and performed in all manner of films before deciding to settle down with Westerns. In McCrae's case, the decision had much to do with his own off-camera life as a rancher. McCrae, a man with a charming, easy-going manner, rode horses with graciousness and always seemed in perfect harmony with those spectacular, wide-open spaces. His 1951 picture *Cattle Drive* is a case in good point.

Here he is a cattleman who comes across a spoiled brat (Dean Stockwell) lost in the Arizona rangelands and hauls the boy along with him instead of taking him to the nearest railroad station. In doing so, he tames the arrogant youngster and returns him to his father a much better son.

When making Westerns, Joel McCrae looked for unusual stories. This was one of them — and as with *all* of them, it was his casual but thoroughly believeable presence that gave them such authority. If the men of the real Wild West did not really look like Joel McCrae, then they *should* have.

The American Indian has not fared well in the Western, mostly because he served in the convenient role of villain — or at least as opposition to the white man's progress westwards. Occasionally, there have been films that tried to redress the balance a little. One of them was *Battle at Apache Pass*, which is notable for Jeff Chandler's fine characterization of the wise Apache chieftain Cochise, who led his people to live in peace with the settlers in the Arizona territory following the bloody conflicts that were mostly the result of white greed and treachery.

Battle at Apache Pass with Jeff Chandler as Cochise (left).

Audie Murphy came to film fame as the result of his prominence as America's most decorated soldier of World War II. Under contract to Universal, he settled down to become the studio's top Western star of the 1950's and 1960's. Of particular interest in his series of well-produced Westerns is *Walk the Proud Land* (1956), which featured Murphy in the role of John Philip Clum, the Indian agent who was responsible for the surrender of the feared Apache leader Geronimo. Clum was appointed the agent at the San Carlos Reservation in 1874 during the difficult period when Washington, D. C., was ending military jurisdiction over Arizona and encouraging self-government among the Indians. Clum was the man who worked hardest to bring that about; *Walk the Proud Land* is the film that does the most to point it out.

Glenn Ford's long career has been neatly divided between being a star of all types of movies and a star of superior Westerns. One of them was Universal's 1953 account of *The Man From the Alamo*, based upon the belief that there was one member of the 1836 conflict in San Antonio, Texas, who did not die when the Mexican Army wiped out the garrison of the Alamo. The theory is that he was sent out just before the battle to warn people of what was about to happen; but that he was, thereafter, branded a cowardly deserter. The film traces his final successful efforts to reverse that verdict and gives Glenn Ford ample opportunity to display the cool and likeable image of the lone, courageous, and resourceful Westerner. Thanks to actors like Ford and films like *The Man From the Alamo*, the image is well carved for posterity.

Walk the Proud Land: Pat Crowley, Audie Murphy and Charles Drake.

Glenn Ford punching Hugh O'Brien in *The Man From the Alamo.*

Ronald Reagan's desire to appear in Westerns did not come to fruition until the later years of his film career, despite his ability as a horseman and his interest in ranching. In 1953, Universal offered him the lead in *Law and Order,* which was first made in 1932 with Walter Huston and then again in 1940 as one of the Johnny Mack Brown series. The Reagan version was head and shoulders above the others with Technicolor and good production values.

It is the story of a respected lawman who, after having helped clean up Tombstone, Arizona, retires to the peaceful life of a rancher. He and his wife (Dorothy Malone) move to the town of Cottonwood where he is soon persuaded to put on his badge again when he finds the town dominated by a bad-man (Preston Foster) who hates the lawman because he crippled him in a previous encounter. As in all good Westerns, the law finally gets the upper hand — in this case, thanks to the convincing performance of the gentleman playing the leading role.

Law and Order: Marshall Ronald Reagan on the trail.

Kirk Douglas in *Lonely Are the Brave.*

Lonely Are the Brave (1962) is that rarest of Westerns: a film that comments upon the condition of the individual in a changing society. Kirk Douglas is the movie maverick — a cowboy loner with no respect for the computer age, and content to wander the West at his own speed. He gets himself arrested in order to help a friend break out of jail and then finds that the friend would rather serve his sentence. But the cowboy is not a man to be contained. Douglas makes his break, and it becomes the job of a mild-mannered, compassionate sheriff (Walter Matthau) to track him and bring him to justice. The law has its own way but not until after the cowboy has made some good points about courage, self-reliance, and a man's need to be an individual. Like the man whose story it tells, *Lonely Are the Brave* is very much an individual entry in the Western movie catalog.

Hollywood's long lines of tradition in the making of Westerns have thinned out in recent years, but they have found a champion in Clint Eastwood, who has long gone beyond the limits of superstardom and become an accomplished film maker. He cut his teeth as a Westerner in the television series *Rawhide* in the 1950's and came to fame with the Westerns that he made in Italy. But it was back in Hollywood that Eastwood made Westerns of genuine artistry.

In the case of *High Plains Drifter* (1973), which he also directed, he raised the Western to a kind of Greek tragedy, telling the story of a nameless stranger who arrives in a lawless little town and rids it of its sins. As with so many of the best Westerns, this one is really a morality tale, focusing on the price paid for greed and cowardice. And it is Eastwood, with his cool, aloof, simmering presence that gives the film its strangely compelling quality.

Clint Eastwood as The Stranger in *High Plains Drifter*.

An odd, but wonderful couple: Katharine Hepburn and John Wayne in *Rooster Cogburn*.

And, of course, there is John Wayne. His relationship to the Western is something like Alexander Graham Bell's association with the telephone. Wayne was in the movies for fifty years and maintained star status longer than anybody else. His first ten years were spent starring in dozens of "B" Westerns. But then came director John Ford with *Stagecoach* — and Wayne stepped into film history. He appeared in a variety of pictures, but the lingering image is that of the Westerner.

In 1975, he was teamed with a star of equal legend, Katherine Hepburn, to romp through the starring role of *Rooster Cogburn*. Both stars emerge in full glory: she as a tough, Bible-quoting spinster and he as a pot-bellied, whisky-soaked, one-eyed, old lawman. Against a pair like this, no band of outlaws stand a chance. Neither, fortunately, does an audience.

TIME STEPS AND DOWNBEATS

When Al Jolson yelled, "You ain't heard nothin yet!" in *The Jazz Singer* in 1927, he ushered in the age of the so-called "talking picture." But what he was really doing was introducing moviegoers to a new experience called the movie musical. In those early days of sound, movies did not so much talk as sing — and dance and present hordes of musicians. Within a few years, audiences wearied of this barrage of musicals, and Hollywood soon set its sights on using sound for other than musical purposes.

Each of the major studios came up with a super musical in the form of a revue. These films, now of considerable historic interest, presented all of the talents that the studios then had under contract, plus guest stars. They were little more than elaborate streams of musical numbers interspersed with comedy. In the spring of 1930, Universal hired the great Broadway impresario J. Murray Anderson to direct *King of Jazz* and gave him the then staggering budget of $2,000,000 to dazzle fans. He did just that. When seen today, the film is valuable as a record of former musical stars, particularly Paul Whiteman, the foremost band leader of his day. It was Whiteman who introduced George Gershwin's "Rhapsody in Blue," and that celebrated piece of music is, of course, the highlight of *King of Jazz*.

King of Jazz—Paul Whiteman and his orchestra. This is the first appearance of a major band in a sound film.

Show Boat, the great 1936 version with Paul Robeson, Irene Dunne, Hattie McDaniel, and Helen Morgan.

Show Boat, which opened on Broadway during Christmas week of 1927, had to wait until 1936 before it received respect from Hollywood. By that time, it was firmly established as the foremost American musical of its day, and the songs of Jerome Kern and Oscar Hammerstein II were part of theatrical history. Universal, therefore, had the task of coming up with a *Show Boat* film for which there was a ready and probably critical audience. No one was disappointed.

A five-acre tract along the Los Angeles River was staked out for duplicating a segment of 1880's Mississippi life, and the studio built a replica of a stern-wheeler riverboat upon which to stage the action. Irene Dunne was hired to play the leading role of Magnolia; Charles Winninger played her affable father, Captain Andy; and young tenor Allan Jones was the charming gambler Gaylord Ravenol, who almost breaks Magnolia's heart. But the real casting coups of this version of *Show Boat* were two singers who became legends in American theatrical lore: the magnificent, black, bass-baritone Paul Robeson, whose singing of "Ol' Man River" has never been equalled; and Helen Morgan, a beautiful actress with a plaintive and sorrowful air who singlehandedly set the style for torch singing. Both she and Robeson made their marks in the stage version, and their appearances in the film are just two of many reasons that the 1936 *Show Boat* is a classic movie musical.

Deanna Durbin's film career spanned exactly a dozen years — from 1936 to 1948 — and those years form a special chapter in the history of Universal Pictures. Deanna was *The* Musical Star at Universal; the success of her first movie, *Three Smart Girls,* came at a time when the studio needed an upturn in its fortunes. Deanna proved to be just what

Deanna Durbin, the 14-year-old singing sensation of 1936.

In *Three Smart Girls Grow Up* (1939), Deanna's teacher is played by Felix Bressart.

the doctor ordered. By 1940, she was the highest paid woman in the industry. She was under contract at the age of fourteen for a number of reasons: she was bright, sparkling, and she had a one-in-a-million singing voice — a pure, lyric soprano sound of incredible tone and clarity. *Three Smart Girls* was a case of public love at first sight; and Universal followed it with a more ambitious production, *One Hundred Men and a Girl.* The 100 men are unemployed musicians, one of whom is her father. The enterprising Deanna manages to get the great conductor Leopold Stokowski to conduct them, resulting in employment. This movie, too, proved to be a box-office winner, and from then onwards, the skillful crafting of Durbin musicals became a Universal specialty.

There came a time when Deanna Durbin had to be kissed on screen. It happened in 1939 in the aptly titled *First Love.* The chosen fellow was 21-year-old Robert Stack, whose own association with Universal turned out to be long and profitable.

In 1940 came *Spring Parade,* a true Viennese operetta. Composer Robert Stolz left Vienna because of the war; among the music that he wrote in America was the score for this film, possibly the best of the Durbin musicals. Hitherto, she had always played the vivacious all-American girl. Here she was cast as a lovely Austrian peasant who falls in love with a military bandsman (Robert Cummings), a budding composer, and helps him become a hit. She also becomes friendly with Emperor Franz Josef (Henry Stephenson).

Deanna Durbin's first and only film in Technicolor was *Can't Help Singing* (1944), which was also the most lavishly produced of her films. A Western centered around a wagon trek through spectacular scenery, it displays Deanna as a spirited society beauty tamed by a handsome wagonmaster (Robert Paige). In this film, the singing is what really matters. *Can't Help Singing* was the last score written by the great songwriter Jerome Kern, and it also proved to be the highwater mark in Deanna's career. She made another six movies, but they did not have nearly the same impact as her first six movies.

In 1948, Deanna lowered the curtain on her film career. As few movie stars have ever done, she simply decided to leave Hollywood and stop being an entertainer. Today, the image of Deanna Durbin is indelible; hers is one of the most nostalgic names in Hollywood history.

Can't Help Singing — the only Durbin film in Technicolor. It also has the advantage of a musical score by Jerome Kern and support from Robert Paige, Leonid Kinskey, Akim Tamiroff, and David Bruce.

You're a Sweetheart brought the glamorous Alice
Faye to Universal in 1937 and provided her with
another hit in a long line of musicals that stretched
from the mid-1930's to the mid-1940's when she
decided, to the consternation of millions of admirers,
to retire from the screen. Hers was a throaty, sultry
kind of singing; and a low-key sexiness made her
distinct. *You're a Sweetheart* was a typical, frenetic
backstage musical with Ken Murray as a glib producer
forever getting his star (Alice) in embarrassing
publicity stunts. George Murphy is a waiter mistaken
for a backer, but he is really a dancer looking for a
chance to prove himself. He gets it, of course. And
also gets Alice. The title song became the main hit of
the picture and also served as an elaborate dance
number for Alice and George Murphy. For Faye
connoisseurs, the most memorable few minutes have
to be those when she leans against a pillar and
warmly intones, "So This is Love."

For *You're a Sweetheart* with George Murphy, Universal
borrows the divine Alice Faye from 20th Century-Fox.

And for *If I Had My Way*, Universal borrows Bing Crosby from Paramount.
Sitting next to Bing is Gloria Jean; at the right is Charles Winninger.

Bing Crosby made one of his most pleasant
musicals at Universal in 1940. The studio had
contracted teenaged Gloria Jean because she had a
lyric soprano voice and might, therefore, be a
possible replacement for Deanna Durbin if Deanna
decided to leave or become difficult (which she did
not). Gloria was cast with Bing in *If I Had My Way*
as an orphan on the loose.

A pair of traveling vaudevillians (Bing and the
delightful Charles Winninger) take her to New York to
help find her relatives; but she ends up joining them
in their act, a plot device that allows for a lot of
singing. The famous title song is sung to Gloria by

Bing on the moonlit Hudson River. Together, they
knock off some jaunty numbers like "The Pessimistic
Character With the Crab Apple Face" and "Meet the
Sun Half-Way." All of the songs from the score were
recorded by Bing for Decca; but what makes *If I Had
My Way* especially memorable is the finale, set in a
night club, in which five of the most famous names in
vaudeville appear as guests: Eddie Leonard, Blanche
Ring, Trixie Friganza, Grace LaRue, and Julian
Eltinge. These were veteran stars of the heyday of
vaudeville, and they provide a very good reason to
look at this fine musical.

The Andrews Sisters—La Verne, Maxene, and Patty—doing "Rhumboogie" in *Argentina Nights*, the first of their many Universal pictures.

To review the movie musicals made during the years of the Second World War and not mention the Andrews Sisters is almost like not mentioning Pearl Harbor. The songs they sang and the style in which they sang them are immediately evocative of those years. Patty, Maxene, and La Verne Andrews devised their own harmony and caught the public fancy in 1937 with their recording "Bei Mir Bist Du Schöen." Universal brought them to Hollywood in 1940 to appear in *Argentina Nights,* which resulted in a contract and further appearances in ten other Universal musicals throughout the war years.

Perhaps the best of these films was *In the Navy*

(1941), which starred Abbott and Costello as a pair of woefully inadequate gobs. The studio prefaced the picture with the warning, "Any resemblance between this and an actual career in the United States Navy is purely coincidental." It also starred Dick Powell, then one of Hollywood's most popular singing stars, giving him the role of a radio crooner so sick of female adulation that he escapes into the Navy under another name. *In the Navy* is by far the most musical of the Abbott and Costello comedies and is highlighted by four numbers delivered by the Andrews Sisters, the most memorable of which is the jive song "Gimme Some Skin."

For *In the Navy*, Bud Abbott and Lou Costello need the musical services of Dick Powell and Dick Foran.

Donald O'Connor made his movie debut in 1937 at the age of twelve years and soon became a full-time entertainer — and he still is. He was signed by Universal in 1942 and given star billing in a series of modest musicals; most of them teamed him with Peggy Ryan. The two of them were the studio's juvenile leads throughout the mid-1940's, almost always in pictures about college life or show business. Both were pleasingly comedic players, stressing the antic side of teenage life, particularly the energetic dancing of the period such as the jitterbug. It was soon apparent that O'Connor was an exceptional dancer.

After leading roles in several movies, he was given top billing in *Mr. Big* (1943), which proved to be an apt title. The story tells of college students who resent having to stage a Greek tragedy as the school play and who, thanks to the irrepressible Donald, turn it into a swinging musical. It just so happens that there is a Broadway producer in the audience and . . . guess what?

The film was promoted with the line, "Packed solid with jive that is solid with hepcats." It certainly was solid with moviegoers and resulted in a string of musicals starring Donald O'Connor.

Peggy Ryan and Donald O'Connor in *Mr. Big*, the first of their nine Universal musicals together.

The showbiz story is always a safe bet as background for a musical, especially if it is set in New York City around the turn of the century. Universal mined that vigorous setting in 1944 with *Bowery to Broadway*. With a title like that, the way is open for lots of grand old songs and dances, plus some new ones, and plenty of humorous rivalry between showmen. Jack Oakie and Donald Cook play such a pair, always upstaging each other until they have the sense to become partners and produce shows together. In the meantime, the film treats the viewer to a string of numbers ranging from vaudeville to operetta. Louise Albritton, one of the loveliest actresses ever to grace the sound stages of Universal, increased the merits of *Bowery to Broadway* by turning up in the guise of the celebrated Lillian Russell.

Bowery to Broadway: Jack Oakie, Louise Albritton (as Lillian Russell), and Donald Cook.

Every studio has at least one all-star wartime musical. Universal has *Follow the Boys* with George Raft organizing the Hollywood Variety Committee and recruiting all manner of stars.

The years of the Second World War were incredible ones for American entertainment with a colossal outpouring of productivity and generous attitudes toward entertaining the Armed Forces. Men and women in the services were royally treated at the Hollywood Canteen and all of the other canteens across the country. Stars gladly went anywhere in the world to entertain the troops. A number of movies touched upon those themes; the biggest of them was *Follow the Boys* (1941), which ran a full two hours and included every star at Universal plus Jeanette MacDonald, Artur Rubinstein, Marlene Dietrich, Orson Welles, Dinah Shore, W. C. Fields, and a half dozen orchestras.

In order to string together this massive amount of talent, the studio invented a plot line about a dancer (George Raft) who is turned down by the services for medical reasons but who then becomes one of the most active members of the Hollywood Victory Committee and helps organize shows. Of the more than twenty songs in the film, "I'll Walk Alone" hit an immediate public response; and it lingers as a reminder of those times. *Follow the Boys* defies criticism. It is a record of Hollywood in its glory years — a time and a kind of film that are no more.

Perhaps the most memorable act in *Follow the Boys*—the magic of Orson Welles, himself an amateur magician.

For *The Glenn Miller Story*, James Stewart not only contrives to look like Miller, but learns how to expertly handle a trombone.

It is doubtful if any American band leader occupies a more affectionate spot in the annals of music than Glenn Miller, whose story is told in the appearance of James Stewart in 1954. Miller created a new sound in dance music, a superior sound due to his arrangements and taste; and he became a legend as a result of his work with the Army Air Force Band during the years of the Second World War. He disappeared in late 1944 while flying over the English Channel, but his name and the sound of his music go on and on.

The Glenn Miller Story traces his early days as a trombonist after leaving the University of Colorado and his gradual progress as an arranger with a distinctly personal style. Universal called upon the talents of many famous musicians who associated with Miller: Louis Armstrong; Gene Krupa; Ben Pollack; and his bandsmen and vocal group, "The Modernaires." The results are irresistible.

Nobody going to see *The Benny Goodman Story* in 1955 had any reason to be disappointed, not with the maestro himself doing the actual clarinet playing while the multi-talented Steve Allen supplied the image. Allen was a good choice because of his fair resemblance, and his experience as a musician and composer. The film offers a good account of the career of America's most popular clarinetist-band leader, and also called upon the willing services of his celebrated colleagues in the musical community — people like Harry James, Gene Krupa, Lionel Hampton, Ziggy Elman, Ben Pollack, Teddy Wilson, and Kid Ory. The restaging of highpoints in

Goodman's career allowed for the reprising of many well-loved compositions in the history of the world's music fund. Anyone with any doubts about that need only see *The Benny Goodman Story*.

For *The Benny Goodman Story*, Steve Allen, a solid musician in his own right, learns how to fake the clarinet. In this scene re-creating the Carnegie Hall Jazz Concert of 1938, Steve is joined by Gene Krupa on drums.

Rodgers and Hammerstein's *Flower Drum Song* with Nancy Kwan.

Of the ten musicals written for Broadway by Richard Rodgers and Oscar Hammerstein II, seven were turned into equally successful movies. Univeral acquired the rights to *Flower Drum Song* in 1960 and took advantage of its San Francisco settings, particularly the Chinese community and Grant Avenue, which became the scene of the lively song of that title. The dramatic theme of the story, the generation gap, was heightened by the fact that the families concerned were Chinese with the additional gap of old world traditions and new world values.

But as with all Rodgers and Hammerstein stories, the audience expects and gets a string of beautiful melodies and warm lyrics. Here they range from the philosophical "A Hundred Million Miracles" and "I Enjoy Being a Girl" to the sadly romantic "Love Look Away." *Flower Drum Song* takes its place among the most touching and unusual musicals.

Thoroughly Modern Millie: James Fox and Julie Andrews do "The Tapioca."

Julie Andrews made her Broadway bow in 1954 in *The Boy Friend*, a charming spoof on the Roaring Twenties. A dozen years later, producer Ross Hunter gave Julie a much more elaborate treatment in the same time frame in *Thoroughly Modern Millie* (1967). Hunter knew his stuff.

Here is Julie as an innocent girl from a small town who goes to wild New York City, bobs her hair, and becomes a flapper. She and her lovely orphan friend (Mary Tyler Moore) live in a hotel run by a wacky lady (Beatrice Lillie) who is actually a supplier for the white slave trade. Millie has trouble romancing her handsome boss (John Gavin); and she is herself bothered by a nutty, Joe College type (James Fox). They are all invited to a party at the lavish Long

Island estate of a wild widow (Carol Channing), who turns out to be the mother of the orphan *and* the Joe College fellow. He finally wins the love of Millie while her boss weds the orphan, who isn't an orphan any more.

Such is *Thoroughly Modern Millie* reduced to its bare bones. The meat on those bones is provided by a string of merry songs and dances, some madcap antics and chases, and some thoroughly agreeable performances by Julie Andrews, Mary Tyler Moore, Carol Channing, and James Fox doing a take-off on Harold Lloyd in his heyday as the nice accident-prone young man who amazingly survives all mishaps.

The wide-ranging talents of Shirley MacLaine found a superb vehicle in *Sweet Charity* (1969). The same can be said of director-choreographer Bob Fosse, one of the most vibrant men in the history of the American musical. The good-hearted lady of the title is a dance hall hostess in New York City, a woman who seemingly gets short-changed no matter how good her intentions. She describes herself as "caught in the flypaper of life." Within the space of two hours and forty minutes, and with the imaginative use of 70mm Panavision cameras, Fosse gives the audience a whirlwind account of her adventures as she is taken advantage of by one man after another.

Fosse gathered together a team of expert dancers, all of whom had worked with him before. Some of the highlights: "I'm a Brass Band" with Shirley and a military formation erupting from the fountains of Lincoln Center, dancing across Manhattan, and ending up on Wall Street; the exuberant "If My Friends Could See Me Now" with Shirley doing a dynamic vaudeville song-and-dance; and "Rhythm of Life" with Sammy Davis, Jr., doing a musical sermon in an underground garage complete with hippie chorus whipping up a revivalist fervor.

A visually stunning musical full of Fosse vim and vigor, *Sweet Charity* is perhaps the ultimate Shirley MacLaine film because it presents her with so much opportunity to display her considerable talents in acting and music. She sings, she dances, and she acts the part of Charity with every emotion from brassy to poignant. An incredible lady.

Sweet Charity with Shirley MacLaine and John McMartin.

In a very unusual biblical depiction, *Jesus Christ, Superstar*, Ted Neeley as Jesus confronts his apostles.

The last days of Christ on earth have been the subject matter for many dramatic interpretations, but none more bizarre than the musical *Jesus Christ Superstar,* which director-producer Norman Jewison brought to the screen in 1973. The rock opera ran for two years on Broadway, creating both controversy and rave followings. Jewison kept to the body of the stage original, but he was able to supply far greater visual treatment by filming in Israel and using the Todd-AO photographic process. As with the Broadway version, the film uses largely unknown talent — a wise decision since famous faces would lessen the film's credibility. Two of the original cast members were used in the film: Yvonne Elliman as Mary Magdalene and Barry Dennen as Pontius Pilate. The crucial title role went to Ted Neeley, who received generally good reviews.

But such an unorthodox treatment of Biblical material as this — not only a musical treatment but one styled in contemporary musical terms — cannot by reviewed only on purely personal reactions. The traditionalists may object, but the fact remains that *Jesus Christ Superstar* has touched millions of young people othewise not touched by religious traditions. At first jolt, it may seem irreverent; but in essence, the film is both respectful and impressive.

A musical with a title like *Xanadu* (1980) would have to be different. It is. It spends part of its time up on heaven and the rest on roller skates in southern California. But its real distinction lies in bringing together two delightful talents: the lovely Olivia Newton-John of contemporary music fame and Gene Kelly, stalwart dancer of Hollywood's Golden Age.

Kelly plays a clarinetist who dreams of opening his own nightclub; Olivia is the visiting spirit of Terpsichore, the Greek muse of dancing. She and some of her heavenly sisters stop off to do some skating in Venice (the suburb of Los Angeles) where she meets Kelly and his penniless young artist friend (Michael Beck). She inspires both of them to fulfill their dreams. The boy becomes a successful painter, and Kelly opens up a nightclub called "Xanadu" (actually the Pan Pacific Auditorium in Hollywood).

These flights of fancy are beautifully supported by marvelous special effects and animation, but Xanadu's real charms are its two stars — the shy, beguiling Olivia and Kelly, an actor-dancer-choreographer-director who is his own chapter in Hollywood history.

Xanadu with Michael Beck, Gene Kelly, and Olivia Newton-John performing "There's Gonna Be a Party All Over the World."

Coal Miner's Daughter with Sissy Spacek as Loretta Lynn and Tommy Lee Jones as her supportive husband.

Movie musicals have come a long way since their light and fluffy early days. Now a musical can take a more realistic look at life, as was the case with *Coal Miner's Daughter* (1980), which won Sissy Spacek an Oscar for her portrayal of country singer Loretta Lynn. A true rags-to-riches story, it shows Loretta's origins in a grimy Kentucky town and rescue from poverty by a man (Tommy Lee Jones) who not only makes her his teenage bride, but who encourages

her musical talent. Her charm and voice gradually make her a success, but she finds that life at the top in show business has its own pressures and that they put a strain on personal happiness.

Adapted from Loretta Lynn's autobiography and filmed on location in Kentucky and Tennessee, *Coal Miner's Daughter* is a touching account of a remarkable woman and her music, a story made luminous by the performance of Sissy Spacek.

In *Coal Miner's Daughter*, Beverly D'Angelo plays the tragic Patsy Cline.

HEARTBEATS

———✼———

omance. It would have been impossible for Hollywood to thrive as a provider of popular entertainment had it decided to ignore romance, possibly the most basic of all ingredients in movie-making. Ever since the cameras first started to roll, scriptwriters have wracked their brains trying to think of every angle from which to approach the subject of love and the relationships between men and women whether they be comic, tragic, or something between. Universal did well in the 1930's with films like *Back Street, Imitation of Life*, and *The Magnificent Obsession* — so well that these films are classics of their own kind and dealt with elsewhere in this book.

In January, 1936, Universal released a film that typifies the screen romances of the day: *Next Time We Love,* which stars the enchanting Margaret Sullivan and a young man tackling his first leading role in the movies, James Stewart. The film touches upon a problem that was gradually gaining attention in American life — a woman's choice between career and marriage. Here Sullivan is an actress and Stewart is a successful newspaperman whose assignments take him out of town, but his wife refuses to travel with him. Besides, she wants success of her own. Will their love overcome their problems? In 1936, there wasn't much doubt that love conquers all.

Next Time We Love: James Stewart and Margaret Sullivan.

Maria Montez, a sultry, exotic beauty from the Dominican Republic, had been at Universal for about a year and a half doing small roles in nine films before producer Walter Wanger had the inspired idea of starring her in *Arabian Nights* in 1942. In doing so, he found not only the right niche for her, but also a winning streak for the studio. For the next four years, Maria became Universal's Queen of Adventure Fantasies, the titles of which are explanation enough: *White Savage, Ali Baba and the Forty Thieves, Cobra Woman, Gypsy Wildcat, Sudan,* and *Tangier.*

Although an actress of very limited range, she had an almost hypnotic presence on the screen, part of which was surely due to the obvious pleasure she took in making these highly colored comic-strip epics. After seeing *Arabian Nights,* she was quoted as saying, "When I look at myself, I am so beautiful, I scream with delight," a remark that registered her either as Hollywood's most narcissistic star or as one with a tremendous flair for publicity. Probably both.

With her thick Latin accent, her sensual movements, and her eye-popping wardrobe, Maria Montez cut a figure that beautifully fitted the wartime need for escapist entertainment. Her vanity, however, proved tragic. She exercised and dieted severely to keep her weight down and died from a heart attack at the age of 32 years. It was generally thought that her career had run its course; yet, her name still has a touch of magic, and those incredible fantasy movies of hers still excite her old fans and even find new ones.

Arabian Nights with Maria Montez and Jon Hall.

By 1945, Universal sensed that Maria Montez' popularity might slip with the postwar years and that it would be wise to find a similarly exotic beauty, but one with a possibly wider range of talent. They chose 22-year-old Yvonne DeCarlo from Vancouver, British Columbia, and starred her in the lavish *Salome, Where She Danced.* Yvonne had already had bit parts in twenty films, enough of an apprenticeship to make her step to stardom fairly smooth. She was also less temperamental than Montez and more capable. She slithered through exotic romps like *Song of Scheherazade* and *Slave Girl,* and lusty Westerns like *Frontier Gal* and *Black Bart,* in which she played Lola Montez; but she also did well when given dramatic roles in *Brute Force* and *Criss Cross.* In time, Yvonne demonstrated even more ability with a variety of movies made in various parts of the world and with her appearances in night clubs and stage musicals.

In 1964, she returned to Universal as one of the stars of the popular television series *The Munsters,* winding up with a feature film version — *Munster, Go Home* — two years later. In 1971, she was one of the stars of the Broadway musical *Follies* and brought down the house each evening with the song "I'm Still Here." No better comment could be made about the durable Yvonne DeCarlo.

Salome, Where She Danced: Rod Cameron and Yvonne DeCarlo.

Tony Curtis as *The Prince Who Was a Thief.*

Tony Curtis was 24 years old when he was put under contract by Universal in 1949 and carefully nurtured into stardom. Because of his New York accent, he was not a logical choice for costumed adventure films; yet, those pictures turned out to be some of his most popular early successes. His striking looks, charm, and good-humored sense of mock-heroics more than compensated for his accent.

The Prince Who Was a Thief was a box-office winner in 1951. Here, Curtis is a robber lad in old Arabia falling in love with a lovely young street dancer (Piper Laurie) whose own theft of royal jewels brings suspicion on the lad, but also leads to the revelation that he is actually a member of the royal household. As can only happen in stories of this nature, she also ends up as his bride. With *The Prince Who Was*

a Thief, Tony Curtis became Hollywood royalty.

The Black Shield of Falworth is, more or less, an Arabian Nights yarn set in fifteenth century England. In this film, Tony Curtis is a lusty young peasant who, because of his bravery, is made a cadet of the royal armory. He flirts with a lovely young noblewoman (Janet Leigh — then Mrs. Curtis) but fails to be taken seriously because of his social standing. However, it evolves that the gallant young man is really the son of a dishonored knight, which then makes the romance acceptable, especially after he dispatchs the villain (Derek Farrar) who tarnished his father's name, a deed that also saves the kingdom from the villain's planned takeover. Such is the stuff of *The Black Shield of Falworth,* a solid hit in the Tony Curtis catalogue.

A few centuries later in medieval England, Tony Curtis is a squire in *The Black Shield of Falworth*, in company with Leonard Mudie, Rhys Williams, and Barbara Rush.

To be effective and not ridiculous, romantic melo-dramatics need to be carefully handled. An excellent case in point is *Written on the Wind* (1956), firmly directed by the esteemed Douglas Sirk. The story is laid amid the wealthy set in Texas with Rock Hudson as the friend and employee of playboy-oilman Robert Stack, whose loneliness has led him to alcoholism and whose sister (Dorothy Malone) has turned into a nymphomaniac because of her unrequited love for Rock. The playboy straightens up when he marries a New York secretary but starts to drink again when he learns that she is pregnant. Since he is sterile, he assumes the child is that of his friend (Rock), whom

he tries to kill. But in the subsequent melee, it is the playboy who ends up dead. The testimony given by the sister clears Rock of blame, even though she knows in doing so that she is clearing the path for him and the widow to find happiness together, the kind of happiness that just doesn't seem to be her lot.

Written on the Wind presents this torrid material with great style. Dorothy Malone won an Oscar for her performance as the beautiful but distressed sister; and the always reliable Robert Stack received critical approval for his playing of what could have been a ludicrous role in the hands of a lesser actor.

Written on the Wind: Rock Hudson, Lauren Bacall, Robert Stack, and Dorothy Malone.

Tammy and the Bachelor with a young Leslie Nielsen, Debbie Reynolds, and Walter Brennan.

Tammy and the Bachelor (1957) proved to be a highlight in the career of Debbie Reynolds, made more so because of the song written for the film by Jay Livingstone and Ray Evans, which became always identified with her. Tammy is a nice Southern country girl thrust by circumstance into the company of wealthy, snobbish people. Because of her basic values, she shows up the snobs, one of whom (Leslie Nielsen) she wins as a husband. Set in the Bayou country of Mississippi, ranging from life on a modest houseboat to life amid the landed gentry of the plantations, *Tammy and the Bachelor* found a wide audience and a demand for more pictures about this charming young lady of the Old South.

Debbie Reynolds decided not to do the sequel, so that part went to Sandra Dee, who turned out to be equally charming. *Tammy Tell Me True* (1961) forgot about the marriage of the previous picture and put Tammy back on the riverboat but with the realization that she needs higher education. It, plus romance, comes in the form of a handsome teacher (John Gavin).

In Tammy Tell Me True, Sandra Dee turns into Tammy, who has the attention of John Gavin.

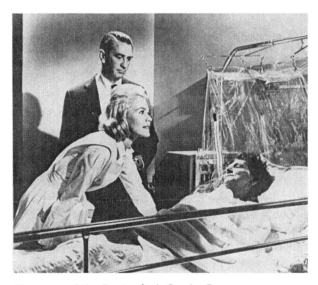

Tammy and the Doctor finds Sandra Dee as a nurse, along with Beulah Bondi as a patient and Macdonald Carey as a doctor.

Two years later, Sandra Dee agreed on another Tammy outing — *Tammy and the Doctor*, but she declined to do the *Tammy* television series started in 1965.

The battle of the sexes is ever-open territory for writers of comedy; and in 1959, Universal hit a new high with *Pillow Talk*. A great deal of the impact comes from the felicitous casting of Doris Day and Rock Hudson. She had long been one of America's most appealing singing actresses, but this film put her onto an even higher plane — as it also did for Hudson. He had been signed by Universal in 1949 and carefully guided through years of build-up with parts in a variety of pictures, eventually playing leads in Westerns and adventure films.

By 1959, he was a safe bet for *Pillow Talk*, playing a Manhattan wolf who spends a lot of time on the telephone warming up his intended dates.

Unfortunately, the lady in the next apartment (Doris), an interior designer, has to share the same phone line and can rarely get to use it. When he meets her, he finds her to be a knockout; but in order to woo her, he has to assume another identity since she has only contempt for the man who shares her party line. Many bits of comedic business come and go before the final blending of Doris and Rock, but it is the flair and style of those bits of business that made *Pillow Talk* a box office smash in 1959 and won an Oscar for Best Original Screenplay. Doris Day was nominated for an Oscar for Best Actress but lost to Simone Signoret.

Rock Hudson, Tony Randall, and Doris Day in *Pillow Talk*.

Encore! Doris and Rock in *Lover Come Back*.

The sucess of *Pillow Talk* made a re-teaming of Day and Hudson inevitable, but two years passed before they were clear of other commitments. *Lover Come Back* did as well for them — and for the public — as the previous film. This time, they were both advertising accountants: she, hard working and ethical; and he, the kind of businessman who resorts to wining, dining, and supplying girls. She reports him to the Advertising Council, but his slick maneuvering gets him off the hook. More such maneuvering gets both of them into several amusing conflicts, but her goodness eventually overcomes his badness; the story happily ends on togetherness.

Another encore! Doris, Rock, and Tony Randall in *Send Me No Flowers.*

The success of *Pillow Talk* and *Lover Come Back* made Doris Day and Rock Hudson two of the most popular stars of the day with more offers than either could accept. It also made them cautious about tackling a third picture together, and they waited until 1964 before deciding on *Send Me No Flowers.* This time, the set-up was a little different. They are a married couple and far from being a wolf, Rock is a hypochondriac, so certain that he is about to expire that he picks a replacement for himself in the form of a great big healthy hulk (Clint Walker). It takes all kinds of ploys to prove to Rock that he is a healthy man himself, with his many medicines consigned to the garbage can.

After *Send Me No Flowers*, Doris and Rock decided not to push their luck any further as a team. They had three winners — better leave it at that.

Any further compliments to Cary Grant are redundant. Suffice it to say that no one has yet come along to replace him. His perfect balance between skill and charm are well displayed in *That Touch of Mink* (1962), which teamed him with Doris Day in yet another variation of the battle of the sexes. In this film, he is a wealthy bachelor intent upon staying one; she is the feisty young beauty who finally gets him to the altar. The 99 minutes between opening and closing are filled with comedic situations, misunderstandings, witty dialogue, stylish sets and costumes, and the work of a pair of expert players in this particular league. The word *mink* in the title could well be changed to *style*.

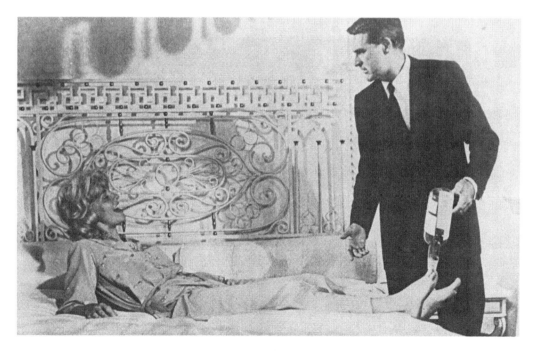

That Touch of Mink, starring Doris Day and Cary Grant.

Cary Grant followed *That Touch of Mink* with *Charade,* this time in the company of a lady whose style and charm lay precisely in his range: Audrey Hepburn. Set in Paris, and with such skill that the city becomes the third star of the film, this picture is about a widow whose murdered husband was involved with crooks and large sums of money, and a man who offers to help her when it looks like she may be the next victim. But is this man actually one of the crooks himself?

The film is not called *Charade* for nothing. And the producers knew exactly the results of pairing Cary Grant with Audrey Hepburn and placing them in an intriguing plot in Paris.

American Graffiti (1973) was the springboard for more careers than possibly any other film in Hollywood history. Among them: producer Francis Ford Coppola; director George Lucas; and actors Richard Dreyfus, Ron Howard, Cindy Williams, Candy Clark, and Harrison Ford. It is one of the most poignantly nostalgic evocations of American lifestyle ever put on the screen. The story takes place in the small California city of Modesto in the early 1960's; during the course of one evening, we see the city's teenagers cruising the streets in their cars. They joke, they quarrel, they flirt, they fight, they fall in and out of love, and they razz the police. Throughout the evening, they keep their car radios tuned to disc jockey Wolfman Jack, who spins all the hits of the time.

Charade and the scene in which Audrey Hepburn asks Cary Grant: "Do you know what's wrong with you?" He: "No, what?" She (dreamily): "Absolutely nothing."

Thanks to its fine script and direction, *American Graffiti* is an almost painfully observed account of what is generally considered to be the twilight of American innocence — before Vietnam, before the drug culture, before shocking political assassinations and campus protests. Adolescence has never been more accurately or lovingly treated than this.

American Graffiti with two youngsters who would become even more successful—Cindy Williams (in the TV series *Laverne and Shirley*) and Ronny Howard (as a movie director).

The Other Side of the Mountain: Marilyn Hassett as Jill Kinmont and Dabney Coleman as her trainer.

In 1955, 19-year-old Jill Kinmont, having won several important ski competitions, had her sights set on the Olympics. But while taking part in the Snow Cup Race, she skied off the side of a mountain and broke her neck. *The Other Side of the Mountain* (1975) is the story of Jill Kinmont (as played by Marilyn Hassett), a girl who was not wiped out by her severe injuries. Despite being paralyzed from the shoulders down, she vowed to recover as much of her bodily functions as she possibly could, eventually gaining limited movement and mobility in a wheelchair. Her rehabilitation with all its mental as well as physical pain is the substance of the film. Her strongest ally is another skier, a charmingly eccentric character named Dick Buek (Beau Bridges), who finally persuades her to marry him. But he is killed in a plane crash before the marriage can take place. In this case, truth is not only stranger than fiction but more tragic, and it accents the courage of this remarkable girl.

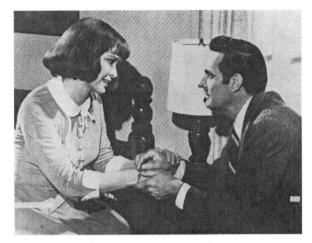

Same Time, Next Year, starring Ellen Burstyn and Alan Alda.

next . . . and the next. Slade's play and film take a look at the couple a half-dozen times over the next quarter-century and note not only their continued love for one another, but their careers, marriages, children, and general development as humans. They maintain a deep and lasting affection without causing pain to anyone else. Therein lies the beauty and the humor of *Same Time, Next Year*.

By the time he made *The Four Seasons* (1981), Alan Alda had proven his talents as an actor capable of everything from comedy to tragedy, and as a writer and a director for television. But here he was able to bring all those talents to bear for the first time with a major feature film that turned into a triumph for him.

His story is an examination of the lifestyles and characters of three upper-middle-class couples who vacation together four times a year. Alda himself is a lawyer of calm disposition and analytical mind. He likes everything to be *just so*. Gradually, he finds that life is not *just so*, especially when one of the

The Four Seasons: Carol Burnett, Beatrice Alda, Jack Weston, Alan Alda, Rita Moreno, Bess Armstrong, and Len Cariou.

Extra-marital romance has long been a reliable staple in the art of story-telling. In Bernard Slade's Broadway play *Same Time, Next Year*, it received a full, tender, and humorous examination. Slade himself was the scriptwriter when his play was made into a movie in 1978, and he could hardly have hoped for a better pair of players than Alan Alda and Ellen Burstyn.

The story is that of newlyweds who meet at a California resort while vacationing without their spouses. They fall in love but not enough to break up their marriages — just enough to want to meet again at the same time the following year. And the

couples divorces, and the ex-husband brings his new girlfriend into the group. The situation causes some revision and eventually a stronger assessment of the friends' regard for each other. *The Four Seasons* is a touching and expert review of the modern American way of life.

Writer-director Alda was wise enough to surround himself with such talents as Carol Burnett, Jack Weston, Sandy Dennis, and Rita Moreno. Players like these people are comparable to the members of an esteemed orchestra playing the music of Vivaldi's *The Four Seasons*, which is what Alda chose as his background score.

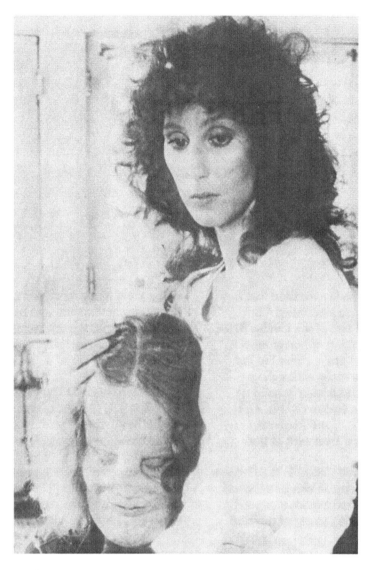

Mask with Cher as the loving mother.

Mask is the true story of Rocky Dennis, an otherwise normal teenager afflicted with a rare disorder resulting in an enlargement of the skull. This touching film, finely directed by Peter Bogdanovich, provided Cher with her best opportunity (until 1985) to prove the range of her dramatic talent. Long popular for her singing and comic ability, what now became apparent was her ability to reveal human frailty and compassion.

As Rusty, the mother of Rocky (Eric Stoltz), she is a bike rider and headstrong woman unable to keep her life in order, but fiercely devoted to her son. Both of them are outcasts — she by her lifestyle and he by his appearance; both are constantly at odds with themselves and others.

Mask is a film of unusual sensitivity; it is to the credit of Bogdanovich that the boy's condition is never made to seem abnormal, and the bikers who make up his family are not treated with the condescension so common in films about this lifestyle.

Since making *Mask,* Cher has demonstrated yet more of her skill as an actress; but it was here that she emerged as an actress with more to offer than had been assumed. Her portrayal is of a troubled mother, yet a fragile woman hovering between toughness and vulnerability, torn between anger and love. A remarkable performance in an affecting film.

FRIGHTFUL!

In 1930, Carl Laemmle made a decision that met with some doubt among his associates. He decided to make a major film of the famous Bram Stoker novel *Dracula*. A number of horror movies had been made in Hollywood in the Silent Era but none of any distinction. The really outstanding examples of that kind of film had been done in Germany — classics like *The Golem* (1914), *The Cabinet of Dr. Caligari* (1920), and *Nosferatu* (1922). The latter was the first treatment of the Stoker novel.

Could Hollywood successfully follow in the German cinematic tradition? Carl Laemmle was sure it could. All through the twenties, he had employed a good deal of German talent; with the coming of the Nazi era, a great many more talented actors, writers, directors, cameramen, and composers found a home at Universal Studios and helped make that studio, more than any other, renowned for the making of horror movies.

Dracula was made in 1930 and released the following year, and whatever doubts the industry had about the American public's acceptance of a film about blood-hungry vampires were immediately swept away. To play the title role, Universal hired Hungarian actor Bela Lugosi, who had already played the part on the stage. He was perfect. Lugosi was both chilling and dapper, elegant and cold, suave and eerie; and his thick, lyrical accent soon became the

Dracula: Bela Lugosi as the Count welcoming Mr. Renfield (Dwight Frye).

stuff of impersonators. To horror buffs, Bela Lugosi *is* Count Dracula.

Dracula is a story of the undead set in Transylvania. It begins in dank, cobwebbed Castle Dracula where a touring Englishman named Renfield (Dwight Frye) goes to meet the Count. When he accidentally cuts his finger, the blood causes Dracula to pounce upon him. Later in England, Renfield is placed in an insane asylum. Dracula follows him and sets himself up in a deserted abbey. His hunger for blood leads him to spot a beautiful girl, Lucy (Helen Chandler), whom he soon has under his power, inciting the anger of her fiance (David Manners), who calls upon the services of an expert on vampires, Dr. Van Helsing (Edward van Sloan). Together, they bring an eventual end to the Count's killings and blood lusts. Finding him in his coffin at dawn, Van Helsing drives a stake through Dracula's heart. At last, after centuries of depravity, the Count is dead. *But is he really?* With the success of this Gothic classic, there was no way that moviemakers were going to allow similar subjects to rest in peace.

Variations of the Dracula story have been filmed many times, but it was not until 1979 that Universal produced a re-make of the Lugosi original. Filmed amid beautifully gloomy locations in England, this *Dracula* has the advantage of magnificent color photography and special effects, and a richly tragic-romantic musical score by John Williams. Handsome Broadway actor Frank Langella makes the Count a much more sexy and beguiling gentlemen, but equally as scary as Lugosi. The gorgeous Kate Nelligan plays the smitten Lucy, and Sir Laurence Olivier gives greater dimensions to the role of Van Helsing. In short, it is a masterpiece of fascinating evil.

The success of *Dracula* paved the way for Universal's next major foray into horror: *Frankenstein* (1931). To play the role of the monster, they chose a mild-mannered English gentleman named William Henry Pratt who had invented for himself the stage name of Boris Karloff. An intelligent actor, Karloff decided to give his huge, lumbering monster a touch of humanity, a vulnerability that causes audiences to feel pity as well as fear.

The story is that of an ambitious scientist (Colin Clive) who seeks to create life artificially and does so by stealing parts of fresh corpses from a cemetary. Unfortunately, his assistant, instructed to steal the brain of a medical student, steals the brain of a criminal. In his laboratory in a deserted watchtower full of strange electrical equipment, Dr. Frankenstein brings his monster to life — and finds that he has truly

created a monster. It kills the assistant who torments it, breaks out of its dungeon, and kills more people in the town. It almost kills the doctor himself, but the townspeople trap the monster in an old mill and burn it, presumably putting an end to the fearful creature. But a monster who did this well at the box offices of the world could hardly be expected to stay dead.

The original *Frankenstein* set a new standard in the art of the horror with its excellent production values, imaginative sets and photography, and fine performances. Apart from the riveting presence of Boris Karloff, *Frankenstein* had two major assets: director James Whale and make-up expert Jack Pierce. Whale brought great taste and skill to this kind of film, creating its eerie atmosphere and suspense with his use of lighting, camera angles, and editing. Pierce was entirely responsible for the look and the shape of the monster, which he was called upon to create many more times. He was also the man who dreamed up the appearances of The Mummy, The Wolf Man, and other frightening creatures for the screen.

Boris Karloff as Frankenstein's monster.

Frankenstein: the controversial scene with the little girl (Marilyn Harris), cut after the first showings but restored in the new cassette version.

In 1932, James Whale was hired by Universal to make another film that would turn out to be a milestone in the horror league: *The Old Dark House.* Again he called upon Jack Pierce and Boris Karloff along with an English actor who had just arrived in Hollywood — Charles Laughton.

It concerns a group of travelers who seek refuge during a storm in the Welsh mountains and find shelter, among other things, in a gloomy mansion owned by an eccentric atheist (Ernest Thesiger) whose mute hulk of a butler (Karloff) becomes murderous when drunk. They also find an insane relative locked up in a wing of the house who, if freed, will burn the house down. He tries, but the travelers manage to kill him before they are subjected to any more of the horrors of *The Old Dark House.* A masterpiece.

The Old Dark House: Raymond Massey, Lilian Bond, Gloria Stuart, Melvyn Douglas, Boris Karloff, Charles Laughton, and Eva Moore—quite a cast.

Boris Karloff and Zita Johann
in *The Mummy.*

Boris Karloff also made *The Mummy* in 1932, yet another weird exercise in dreadful fantasy and another giant step in his career. Here he is a High Priest of ancient Egypt buried alive for stealing sacred scrolls. A British museum unearths the mummy and the scrolls 3,700 years later. The mummy comes alive, poses as an archeologist, and leads an expedition back to Egypt to find the tomb of the princess he loved long ago. As is always the case in stories like this, the scheme goes awry . . . and the audience shudders in delight. There's nothing quite like seeing a man embalmed alive.

Another English gentleman, Claude Rains — he of the crisp manner and soft, distinct diction — made a mark for himself in the annals of Universal horror films with *The Invisible Man* in 1933. Again, it was the guiding hand of director James Whale that gives this film its eerie style and bitter humor.

The H. G. Wells classic of science fiction received an intelligent treatment in telling the shocking story of a research chemist (Rains) who discovers a drug that bleaches animal tissue to transparency, but carries madness as a side effect. The chemist cannot resist the challenge of making himself invisible, realizing the power it would give him; and he takes the plunge without first perfecting an antidote. Frustration leads to madness and murder, and the only time the invisible chemist ever becomes visible is when he lies dying, shot to death by the police.

The Invisible Man pleased the critics with its literate script, and it amazed the moviegoers of 1933 with its trick photography of an invisible body dressing and undressing, and footsteps in the snow made by someone who could not be seen. James Whale clearly knew that what cannot be seen can be scarier than what can be seen.

The Invisible Man with Claude Rains, visible only when completely covered, and Gloria Stuart.

The inevitable reappearance of Boris Karloff as Baron Henry Frankenstein's monster took place in 1935 in *The Bride of Frankenstein*, and James Whale was brought in as director. The result was superior to the original Frankenstein; in fact, *The Bride of Frankenstein* is regarded by most horror film buffs as the finest movie in the whole genre.

The film starts with a scene in which the authoress of the original Frankenstein novel, Mary Shelley (Elsa Lanchester), is encouraged by friends to continue the saga. She devises an escape for the monster from the fire that presumably killed him, and another escape from the jail in which he is placed after capture by the townspeople. Dr. Pretorious (Ernest Thesiger), Baron Frankenstein's teacher, persuades

cially admirable as is the musical score of the recently arrived German composer Franz Waxman, who set a new high standard in providing background music for a horror picture.

Four years passed, and Universal came forth with *Son of Frankenstein*, the son in the form of the chillingly suave Basil Rathbone. The studio heightened the film's appeal by adding Bela Lugosi in the role of the deformed Ygor, a shepherd who escaped death by hanging years before, although this left him with a permanent crick in his neck. When the Baron returns to take up residence in his ancestral home, he stumbles across his father's old laboratory where Ygor tells him that the monster is still alive but

The Bride of Frankenstein: Colin Clive, Elsa Lanchester, Boris Karloff, and Ernest Thesiger.

Dr. Frankenstein to invent a bride for the monster; to this effect, a young woman is killed to gain a heart. The bizarre experiment is a success — up to a point. The invented woman recoils in horror when she sees her intended husband; and he, in a rage of abject disappointment, goes berserk and slaughters everyone with the exception of Dr. Frankenstein, whom he, with a twinge of compassion and gratitude, allows to escape to join his own bride (Valerie Hobsen).

The *Bride of Frankenstein* loses none of its effectiveness with the passage of time. Its sets are espe-

in a coma. To vindicate his father's name, young Frankenstein revives the monster but loses control of him to the evil Ygor, who uses the monster to murder the jurors who sentenced him to hang. In due time, the Baron kills Ygor in self-defense. The offended monster kidnaps the Baron's son; but in the final skirmish, the Baron manages to shove the monster into a pit of boiling sulphur.

Son of Frankenstein marked Boris Karloff's final appearance as the monster, but such was the success of the film that it launched Universal's horror film cycle stretching through the 1940's. Karloff appeared in *House of Frankenstein* (1944) — not as the monster but as a mad scientist. In that production, the monster is played by Glenn Strange; in the *The Ghost of Frankenstein* (1942), it was Lon Chaney, Jr., in the guise of the much misunderstood hulk.

Son of Frankenstein: Edgar Norton, Boris Karloff, Basil Rathbone, and Bela Lugosi.

House of Frankenstein: Boris Karloff, now a mad doctor, settles his score with Count Dracula (John Carradine).

The name Chaney is virtually engraved in Universal history — first, because of Lon Chaney's early years at the studio specializing in roles involving weird make-up often bordering on the horrific; and second, because of his son. Lon Chaney, Jr. was contracted in 1940 to star in *Man Made Monster*, a piece of casting that changed the course of his career. Over the next decade, he becomes *the* star of Universal horror pictures, starting with his most famous role in *The Wolf Man* (1941).

This is the sad story of Larry Talbot (Chaney, Jr.), who returns to his ancestral home in Wales after many years in America, becomes reunited with his father (Claude Rains), and falls in love with a local girl (Evelyn Ankers) from whom he acquires a silver-tipped cane that she tells him symbolizes the legend of the Werewolf. One dark night in the woods, he kills an attacking wolf with the cane and is then astounded to see the body of the wolf turn into the corpse of a gypsy (Bela Lugosi) who had predicted impending disaster. Larry is bitten by the wolf in the encounter. Later, he begins having nightmares, and worse still, slowly starts evolving into the hideous Wolfman when the moon is full. As such, he wreaks havoc and bloody murder until the night when Talbot Senior comes across the beast and beats it to death with the same cane, watching in horror as the dead creature turns back into the corpse of his son.

The Wolfman: Claude Rains as Sir John Talbot and Lon Chaney, Jr., as his son Lawrence . . .
. . . who undergoes a considerable transformation when the wolfbane blooms.

The Wolf Man was an instant hit. Chaney, Jr., not only played the role in four more films, but he also appeared in many of the studio's spin-offs featuring The Mummy, Frankenstein, Dracula, and other monstrous creatures. Much of the effectiveness of *The Wolf Man* was due to hideous make-up; the man responsible for that was the esteemed Jack Pierce.

In recent years, the art of make-up has surpassed anything even Jack Pierce could have imagined, due to new substances and techniques — not to mention trick photography. This was shockingly apparent in *An American Werewolf in London* (1981) in which make-up man Rick Davis devised effects never before seen in a film.

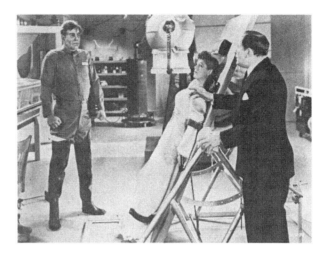

In this Technicolor fantasy, a pair of American students touring the north of England are attacked by a fierce and ugly beast. One is killed and the other is badly mauled. The survivor (David Naughton) is horrified some time later when the deceased student (Griffin Dunne) visits him, warning him to commit suicide or run the risk of turning into a Werewolf. He ignores the advice — with inevitable results. After a number of brutal killings, he is slaughtered in Piccadilly Circus.

Director-writer John Landis won credit for both the horror and the humor of his story, but it is the work of Rick Davis that lingers in the mind — those shots of the deceased student's face rotting in motion and that of the bitten student turning into the Werewolf as we watch — fingers becoming claws, hair sprouting, bones contorting, and the face extending into a huge snout. With *An American Werewolf in London*, the art of the horror film reached a frightening new plateau.

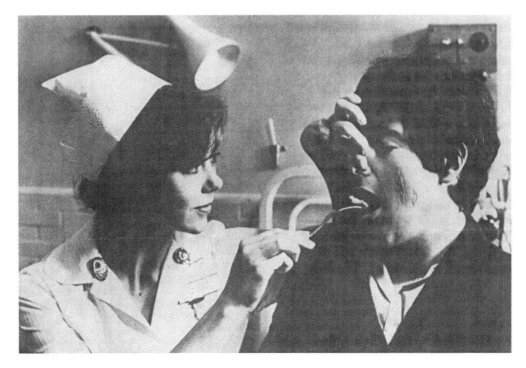

An American Werewolf in London, starring Jenny Agutter and David Naughton.

The Creature from the Black Lagoon: Bernie Glazer protects Julie Adams from the Gill Man, emerging from a lagoon built right in the middle of the Universal backlot.

braves his way into the strange lair and attempts to fight the creature. His life hangs in the balance until the rest of the team arrives and fills the creature full of bullets. The poor beast drags itself back to the lagoon, presumably to die. But does he? Who knows?

The Creature from the Black Lagoon was a hit when it first appeared; over the years, it has become almost a cult item among horror buffs, who seem to have a certain sympathy for the hideous hybrid.

Science fiction blossomed with the Space Age, and Hollywood devised all manner of frightful ways to combine fear with curiosity about the ever-widening borders of technology. *The Incredible Shrinking Man* (1957) tells the alarming tale of a man (Grant Williams) who, while on a boat cruise, sails through a fogbank of radioactive insecticide. He undergoes all kinds of harrowing experiences as he diminishes in size. When down to about two inches in height, the family cat takes after him; and in his wine cellar, he has a fearful encounter with a spider. Eventually, *The Incredible Shrinking Man* shrinks to nothingness. But not at the box office.

The Creature from the Black Lagoon (1954) was among the first horror movies to use the 3-D process, enabling moviemakers to seemingly thrust their frightening effects right into the audience.

The story tells of a scientific expedition up the Amazon and the excitement caused by the discovery of a web-fingered skeleton-fossil that suggests to the scientists that there still exists a creature from the past linking land and water mammals. They hire an expert diver (Richard Carlson), who does, indeed, discover that there exists an ugly half-man, half-fish and that it does not take kindly to being disturbed in its deep domain. In fact, it kills several of the scientists. When it spots the beautiful female member of the team (Julie Adams), the vicious reptile falls in love — and carries her off to his cavern. The diver

In *The Incredible Shrinking Man*, Grant Williams gradually gets smaller and smaller.

Earthquake (1974) proved that horror is not limited to the world of ghosts, ghouls, and imagined monsters. This is about the horror that could overtake the citizens of Los Angeles if a truly major earthquake hit their city. This was also the film that used a disturbing process called "Sensurround," a sound track device that sends sound tremors through the theatre to supplement the scenes of Los Angeles breaking up. Charlton Heston heads the large cast of characters trying to survive the catastrophe, but the real stars of *Earthquake* are the special effects crew. Thanks to them, we see huge buildings crack and crash, dams burst, roads split asunder, and all the facilities of a modern city break down. Now that is really horror!

Earthquake: Charlton Heston and a Los Angeles nightmare.

Most horror films are flights of fantasy, but there is also the kind that deals with reality, particularly war. They may not be listed as horror films, but the effect is even more frightening.

The Deer Hunter (1978) gave moviegoers a savage jolt, a sudden descent into the chaotic, brutal Vietnam War as experienced by three young men from a Pennsylvania steel town — Robert De Niro, Christopher Walken, and John Savage. They are taken prisoner, kept in rat-infested cages, and tortured. All three "survive" the war: De Niro emerges physically and mentally intact, but Walken becomes demented and drug-addicted, and Savage ends up a shell-shocked amputee. *The Deer Hunter* is about real horror.

In *The Deer Hunter*, Robert De Niro and John Savage are prisoners of war in Vietnam experiencing real horror.

So is *Missing* (1982), the true story of a young American's political murder in a revolution-torn Latin American country. His father (Jack Lemmon) arrives in the country and turns to the American Embassy for help in locating the son whom he knows only to be missing. His daughter-in-law (Sissy Spacek), bitter and disillusioned with government and military agencies, joins forces with the father. Together, they learn the shocking truth: that the son was killed with the knowledge of his own government because he had found out too much about plans and policies. *Missing* deals with the brutality of a police state, and director Costa Gravas' scenes of the liquidation of people for political purposes have a sense of horror that no fantasy can match.

Missing, starring Sissy Spacek and Jack Lemmon.

Ghost Story: Douglas Fairbanks, Jr., Fred Astaire, John Houseman, and Melvyn Douglas.

Universal's long association with horror pictures flaired in 1982 with *Ghost Story*, bringing together four veteran gentlemen of Hollywood — Douglas Fairbanks, Jr., Fred Astaire, John Houseman, and Melvyn Douglas — as four New England aristocrats with a dark secret. They also suffer from nightmares and understandably so. They get together regularly to tell each other ghost stories, but they never allude to the fact that they were responsible fifty years previously for the death of a lovely young girl (Alice Krige), who was engaged to one of them. In a lover's tiff, she was knocked out and apparently killed; the four friends conspired to hide the act by putting her body in a car and sinking it in a river. At the last moment, they realized that she was not dead — but it is too late to save her. Now her spirit seems to have returned for revenge and all kinds of unpleasant things start happening.

Ghost Story lives up to its title, and when that car is hauled out of the river fifty years later and the door springs open . . . well, it takes a strong heart not to gasp. Two craftsmen need to be cited for the chilling stylishness of the film: veteran cinematographer Jack Cardiff and make-up genius Dick Smith.

The mingling of horror and sexuality has always been potent, and it found full flower in *Cat People* (1982), starring exotic Nastassia Kinski as a young girl who turns into a panther (literally) when she makes love. The film opens with a sequence in Africa where a tribe performs the ritual mating of a girl with a black leopard. It then switches to New Orleans, where Kinski comes to live with her brother (Malcolm McDowell), who has also been cursed with this strange transformation and who takes a lustful interest in his sister when he turns into a panther. This is the basis of *Cat People*, perhaps the most bizarre of all horror movies; but also, thanks to the artistry of director Paul Schrader, the most erotically poetic and haunting.

Cat People with John Heard and Natassis Kinski.

Conan the Barbarian: Gerry Lopez, Arnold Schwarzenegger, and Sandahl Bergman.

The art of the Gothic comic book fantasy world comes to full fruition in *Conan the Barbarian* (1982) with a star, Arnold Schwarzenegger, who looks as if he had been drawn by one of those 3comic book artists. The huge, incredibly muscular Austrian is the perfect choice to play Conan, a warrior from an historical era of the distant past who, as a child, witnesses the brutal slaying of his parents by the evil warlord Thulsa Doom (James Earl Jones). Young Conan is taken as a slave boy by Doom and turned into a gladiator when he becomes a young man — a fatal mistake for Doom. With his talents as an athletic swordsman and horseman, Conan escapes to roam the world and find adventure. Among his discoveries is a beautiful and muscular lady drifter named Valeria (Sandahl Bergman), who becomes the perfect partner in both love and combat for the wandering Conan. Eventually, he wanders back into the domain of Thulsa Doom to settle an old score.

With blood and brutality galore, *Conan the Barbarian*, richly costumed and lavishly set, turned the already popular Schwarzenegger into a superstar and made sequels in this line of fantasy adventure inevitable — to the delight of producers and public alike.

FUNNY BUSINESS

Audiences and critics were unanimous in their reaction to the 1940 musical *One Night in the Tropics*: the only really good points in its favor were Bud Abbott and Lou Costello, making their film debut after several years of popularity on the radio. Universal lost no time in putting them under a long-term contract, resulting in more than thirty films over the next fifteen years.

Their first feature is still looked upon by many of their admirers as their best — *Buck Privates* (1941). It tied in with President Roosevelt's announcement of the peacetime draft, and America was much amused to see what happened when this pair was called to the colors. If the Army could survive these rookies, then America was safe.

Abbott and Costello were also safe. They were seldom out of the Top Ten at the box office for the rest of the decade. And Universal, which had dealt with comedy on and off all through its history, now acquired its first specialists in the field.

Averaging three movies a year, Abbott and Costello stumbled through just about *every* avenue of American life. After their Army experience came adventures in the Navy and the Air Force; then forays into the supernatural, the Wild West, crime and detection, the upper reaches of high society, and the sports world. Their characterizations never changed. Bud was the slick, fast-talking, abrasive con man; and Lou, the genial, trusting, permanently confused and continually cheated chump.

Their most famous verbal routine, the baseball double talk about "Who's on first?," got a reprise in *Naughty Nineties* (1945). No matter where or when they did it, it worked. It is probably the most durable bit of comedy ever devised.

After exhausting all facets of Americana, Universal sent Abbott and Costello abroad to places like the South Seas, North Africa, and Alaska as well as up in space. Then the studio had the inspired notion of starring them in a string of comedies in which they meet all of the famous horror figures in Universal's history, starting with *Abbott and Costello Meet Frankenstein* (1948). In other ventures, they meet The Invisible Man, Dr. Jekyll and Mr. Hyde, the Killer (Boris Karloff), and The Mummy. By far the best of these films was the first. It is not only a fine comedy, but a first-rate horror film. Bela Lugosi reprised his celebrated account of Dracula; Lon Chaney, Jr., was

Bud Abbott and Lou Costello in their modest debut as supporting players in *One Night in the Tropics* . . .

. . . and then comes overnight stardom with *Buck Privates*. The sergeant is Nat Pendleton.

the Wolfman; and Glenn Strange stepped in as Frankenstein's monster. The special effects are superbly done, and the monsters all play their parts straight. With poor Lou marked as the unwitting contributor of his brain for use in the Frankenstein

monster, the suspense succeeds in being both chilling and funny. For those who have never seen *Abbott and Costello Meet Frankenstein*, it should be put on the *must* list.

The 14th Abbott and Costello comedy, *The Naughty Nineties* (1945), keeps success rolling. The onlookers: Barbara Pepper, Alan Curtis, Joe Sawyer, and Henry Travers.

An A and C box office bonanza: *Abbott and Costello Meet Frankenstein* (1948). What they actually meet is Frankenstein's monster, played by Glenn Strange.

The great W. C. Fields in *You Can't Cheat an Honest Man*, in company with Constance Moore.

The last four major movies of the legendary comedian W. C. Fields were made at Universal, where he was able to gain greater control over his pictures than he had ever had before, which included writing the scripts. Fields was truly a comic unlike any other. He personified human awkwardness — the man always out of step, fumbling and wistfully incompetent. He claimed to hate children, and he was certainly the enemy of all inanimate objects — or the other way around. Fields was a Don Quixote battered by every windmill he tried to attack.

In *You Can't Cheat an Honest Man* (1939), based on a story by Charles Bogle (one of the many names that Fields dreamed up for himself), he is Larson E. Whipsnade, manager of a circus and always on the run from creditors, to say nothing of sheriffs. He is also at the verbal mercy of Charlie McCarthy and Edgar Bergen, the stars of his circus. After making *You Can't Cheat an Honest Man*, Fields was a frequent guest on the Bergen radio show, where writers devised endless ways for Fields and Charlie to insult each other.

My Little Chickadee (1940) has a special place in film history because it co-starred W. C. Fields with another unique personality — Mae West. Fields and West wrote their own screenplay. Here, they are a pair of confidence trickers in the Old West. She fakes a marriage with him, thinking his bag of counterfeit money is real; but substitutes a goat for herself in their nuptial bed when she finds out it is not. He almost gets hung with his crooked gambling while she sets herself up as a schoolteacher but attracts more men than children to her classes. But the crazy plotlines of *My Little Chickadee* barely need any discussion. This is the movie that brought W. C. Fields and Mae West together. Period.

One of the great pairings in Hollywood history: Mae West and W. C. Fields in *My Little Chickadee*.

Fields' next cinematic onslaught, *The Bank Dick* (1940), is generally regarded as his masterpiece. The screenplay is by Mahatma Kane Jeeves (Fields, of course), and it concerns a man who accidentally captures a bank robber and is rewarded with the job of bank detective. As such, he is horribly inept and gets himself involved in borrowed funds. But he accidentally brings another robber to justice, and the reward enables him to replace the funds. And so on. As an introduction to the lunatic art of W. C. Fields, *The Bank Dick* is essential.

Perhaps the best of the Fields comedies: *The Bank Dick* with Jan Duggan as the irate mother and Bobby Larson as the pesky boy.

Never Give a Sucker an Even Break (1941) is based on a story by Otis Criblecoblis (guess who?), but it is not so much a screenplay as seventy minutes of celluloid vaudeville. Basically, it is about a hack writer (guess who?) trying to sell plots to a movie studio and acting out his ideas, which then become the picture the audience is actually watching. But no one, except as a punishment, should be required to summarize *Never Give a Sucker an Even Break*. Sadly, this turned out to be Fields' last starring role. He appeared in four more pictures in small roles, but the crest of his career was reached with these four

films at Universal. He died in 1946, aged sixty-seven, ending a life that was almost as chaotic and convoluted as the parts he played. W. C. Fields was eccentric and at odds with life; but as a humorist, he was incomparable.

Never Give a Sucker an Even Break with Franklin Pangborn as a film producer,
Leon Belasco as a director, and Fields as a would-be scriptwriter.

Ole Olsen and Chic Johnson in *Hellzapoppin*. What else could it be?

Released at Christmastime, 1941, *Hellzapoppin* was a present that moviegoers could never have imagined. They may have heard that Olsen and Johnson were a wacky pair of comics, but they surely had never seen anything like the scatter-brained antics of *Hellzapoppin*. Ole Olsen and Chic Johnson were veteran vaudevillians by the time they hit Broadway in 1938 in their lunatic revue with this bizarre title. It was the kind of show that was never the same two nights running; and that very fact was, therefore, problematic to film and became part of the technique of filming it. The picture starts with a wild scene in Hades as Olsen and Johnson arrive. They then stop the film and yell to the projectionist to run the scene back for them after which they argue with the director about how to make *Hellza-poppin*. He claims that he cannot just film a bunch of crazy gags. In taking such a stand, the director, of course, is playing a losing game. So is the scriptwriter, who ends up being shot by Olsen and Johnson.

Two years later, this incredible pair returned to Universal to make *Crazy House*; the gag this time is that the studio refuses to make another movie with this pair. So they have themselves shot over a wall by a circus cannon and make the picture in spite of the studio, hiring stand-ins of the stars to be their actors. Finally, they rush their product to a movie house for a showing before the executives can stop them. The real executives at Universal were well aware that *Crazy House* was a hit picture.

Crazy House: Olsen, Johnson, and Cass Daley.

In *The Egg and I*, Claudette Colbert is wary of the request made by lady farmer Louise Allbritton, who wants to borrow husband Fred MacMurray to help with her broken generator.

The Egg and I (1947) proved to be exactly what Universal intended it to be: a successful movie version of Betty MacDonald's funny, best-selling book. Claudette Colbert and Fred MacMurray are the sophisticated couple from New York who painfully and amusingly adapt to the rigors of country life, but the film itself paid off in a way that the studio had not expected. In the secondary roles of a truly rustic pair who befriend the city slickers were cast two veteran character performers — Marjorie Main and Percy Kilbride. She was the large, loud, but generous Ma Kettle; and he, half a foot shorter and mild of manner, was Pa Kettle. The Kettles caught the public's fancy, possibly because they had fifteen children and blithely survived all the chaos around them. In 1949, Marjorie Main and Percy Kilbride received, for the first time in their long careers, top billing as Ma and Pa Kettle.

The public response was so favorable that Universal decided on a series, releasing one film a year: *Ma and Pa Kettle Go to Town*, *Ma and Pa Kettle Back on the Farm*, *Ma and Pa Kettle at the Fair*, *Ma and Pa Kettle on Vacation*, *Ma and Pa Kettle at Home*, and *Ma and Pa Kettle at Waikiki*. Shortly after making the last film, Percy Kilbride was injured in a car accident and decided to retire. The studio made two more Kettle pictures; but without him, the series fizzled, and Marjorie Main also decided to retire. But the Kettles had made their mark, and it was a marvelous way for two great character players to wind up their careers.

Ma and Pa Kettle, in the guise of Percy Kilbride and Marjorie Main.

Donald O'Connor's career went into a second phase when Universal starred him in *Francis* in 1950. He had enjoyed almost a decade as a musical performer, but now he proved himself a capable comedic actor. The role was that of a young Army lieutenant who comes across a mule that can talk (the speaking voice belonged to Chill Wills). The mule does more than talk — it gives him secret information about the enemy. It also causes embarrassment for the lieutenant because it refuses to talk when anybody else is around.

Somewhat to Universal's surprise, *Francis* became a smash hit. Then to almost nobody's surprise, it became a series. First came *Francis Goes to the Races* (1951), then *Francis Goes to West Point* (1952), *Francis Covers the Big Town* (1953), *Francis Joins the WACS* (1954), and *Francis Joins the Navy* (1955). The studio wanted to continue the series; but by this time, Donald O'Connor decided he had had enough. The talking mule had upstaged him for the last time.

Mickey Rooney stepped in to do *Francis in the Haunted House*, but it just was not the same relationship any more; the series was dropped. For all that, Francis the talking mule had done rather well for himself.

Francis: Donald O'Connor as the young lieutenant who has a talking mule for a friend.

Bedtime for Bonzo (1951) has become a curiosity item due to the political career of its star, Ronald Reagan, and due to the fact that it teamed him with a chimpanzee. The assumption that it is, therefore, a low or ridiculous point in Reagan's career is a false one because the film is a very amusing comedy; and all the people in it perform well, including the charming chimp.

The story takes place on a college campus with Reagan as a psychology professor who sets out to prove that environment is a more important factor than heredity in both human and animal behavior. That he has a wild time trying to prove his theory is what *Bedtime for Bonzo* is all about. And it can be said that both Mr. Reagan and Bonzo go about their business with conviction.

In *Bedtime for Bonzo*, Ronald Reagan is the psychology professor who tries to rear a chimp as a child, somewhat to the amusement of wife Diana Lynn.

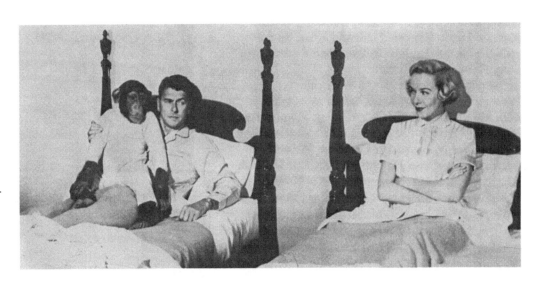

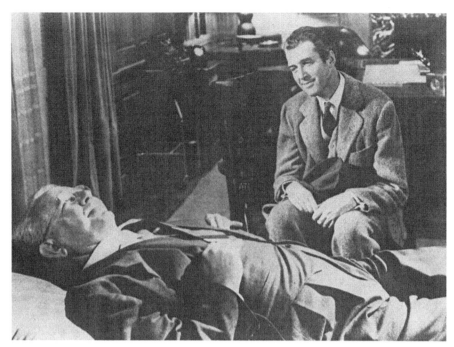

James Stewart as the gentle Elwood P. Dowd in *Harvey*. Such is the charm of Elwood that even psychiatrist Cecil Kellaway takes to the couch to tell Elwood his troubles.

Elwood P. Dowd is a gentle, philosophical soul. He is kind, harmless, and a little off his rocker. His best friend is Harvey, whom he introduces to whomever they come across and with whom he carries on long, pleasant, rambling conversations. The problem is that no one other than Elwood can see Harvey, who is, according to Elwood, a six-foot-tall rabbit. Such is the premise of Mary Chase's play *Harvey*, which was made into a genial movie in 1950. Such is James Stewart's performance as Elwood that it becomes hard for any other actor to play the part without undue comparison. The story calls for Elwood's sister (Josephine Hull) to try getting him assigned to an asylum, but Elwood's sincerity and his sweet nature result in everyone thinking it must be his sister who is not all there. Eventually, she settles for leaving things as they are. How else could a nice, whimsical comedy like *Harvey* end?

Don Knotts plays one of the title characters in *The Ghost and Mr. Chicken* (1966), and it is not the ghost. Knotts has perfected visual nervous anxiety; here, he is at his shivering, quivering best as an

aspiring reporter for a small town newspaper who is assigned to spend a night in a haunted house to write his first story. Torn between ambition and cowardice, the poor man undergoes miseries of fright but turns in a story that wins approval. It also brings a libel suit from the people who own the property — and more shivers and quivers as Don defends himself in court. *The Ghost and Mr. Chicken* is a marathon course for a man who specializes in tying himself in Knotts.

In *The Ghost and Mr. Chicken*, Dick Sargeant tries to persuade would-be writer Don Knotts that there is nothing scary about spending a night in a haunted house.

Burt Reynolds and Sally Fields in *Smokey and the Bandit*.

Smokey and the Bandit (1977) was Hal Needham's first job as a director, and it is easy to see why he was chosen for this wild, wild Burt Reynolds comedy adventure. Needham had long been one of Hollywood's top stunt men and stunt choreographers; *Smokey and the Bandit* needed a man of that particular talent. With the release of this picture, Needham had no further worries about a career as a director. This is a comedy that whizzes along, leaving the viewer gasping between laughs as trucks and cars shoot along Georgia's highways and byways like rockets. It also shot the popularity of the irresistible Burt Reynolds a few light years further into orbit.

In this film, Burt is a racing driver bet by a Texas millionaire (Pat McCormick) and his son (Paul Williams) that he cannot deliver a truckload of illegal beer from one distant point to another in 28 hours. Such an offer is catnip to this daring Southern boy, who does the job with the aid of a wild trucker friend (Jerry Reed). In the process, they raise the blood pressure of pursuing policeman Buford T. Justice (Jackie Gleason). What makes the cop even more furious is that Burt picks up the would-be-bride (Sally Fields) of his dim-witted son (Mike Henry) and runs off with her.

Smokey and the Bandit can hardly be claimed as a course in respect for the law; but as a comedy fantasy and a vehicle for the charming Burt and his stunt buddies, it wins hands down.

However wild and wacky Olsen and Johnson may have been in their heyday, their mouths would probably have dropped open at the antics of college students in *National Lampoon's Animal House* (1978), possibly the most irreverent account of American academic life ever filmed. A satire on the perpetual conflict in today's society between established values and anti-establishment anarchists, the film focuses on the rift between the straight set of Omega House and the fun-loving crowd of Delta Fraternity, who delight in pure hedonism. This includes lots of drinking and over-eating, raids on the girls' dormitories, wild parties, and a general avoidance of anything to do with learning.

Animal House proved to be a box office blockbuster, particularly among the young set who may have been going to college at the time. Undoubtedly, they recognized the targets of some of the academic spoofing. It was also the film that helped John Belushi make his peculiar mark in Hollywood history when he is seen as a glutton sucking up food as a vacuum cleaner gone insane. Slobbery will probably never have a finer exponent than Belushi.

National Lampoon's Animal House, a blockbuster of a comedy with John Belushi as the central, and outrageous, cut up.

Bustin' Loose: Cicely Tyson and Richard Pryor.

With *Bustin' Loose* (1981), Richard Pryor proved himself to be a sensitive actor as well as a man long regarded as a comedian of unusual persuasiveness. In this film, the delightful Richard is a bungling burglar (when not plying his usual trade as a mechanic) who is assigned by his parole officer to aid the prim and proper director (Cicely Tyson) of a school for emotionally disturbed children. Her aim is to transport her charges from the slums of Philadelphia to the calm atmosphere of a farm near Seattle. To

this end, Richard is recruited as the driver of their battered old bus. He is an improbable choice for this odyssey, but he survives the ordeal of shepherding wayward children and finds love with the lady whom he reluctantly sets out to help.

Pryor, with his incredible use of language, both verbal and body, is counterpointed by the delightful Tyson, truly another case of Beauty and the Beast, as the producers of *Bustin' Loose* clearly realized when they cast this contrasting, but appealing pair together.

The Jerk with Jerry G. Velasco, Bernadette Peters, and Steve Martin.

The wild and crazy Steve Martin made a smash movie debut with *The Jerk* in 1979. It pleased his many fans but not the critics. With *Dead Men Don't Wear Plaid* (1981), he succeeded with both groups.

Dealing with the adventures of a far-from-flush private detective called Rigby Reardon (Martin) in the Los Angeles of 1940, it tells of his inept, but nonetheless successful attempts to help a beautiful client (Rachel Ward) find her father's murderers. To this end, he is aided by the likes of Humphrey Bogart and confused by the likes of Alan Ladd, Fred MacMurray, Ava Gardner, James Cagney, Vincent Price, and several other stars of Hollywood's Golden Age.

Directed and partly written by Carl Reiner (who also appears as the principle villain, the leader of a band of Nazis), *Dead Men Don't Wear Plaid* is a triumph of film editing, mixing multiple clips from seventeen vintage movies with shots of Martin and the gorgeous Rachel Ward.

Steve Martin again—this time with Rachel Ward in *Dead Men Don't Wear Plaid.*

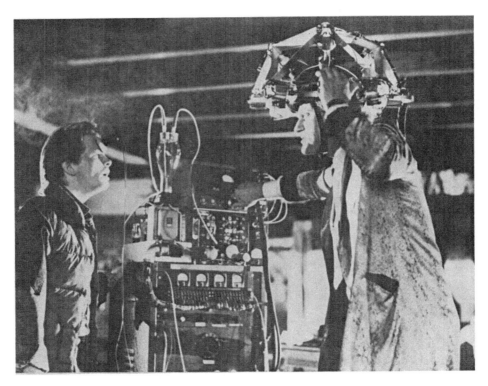

Back to the Future, starring Michael J. Fox and Christopher Lloyd.

Time travel, one of the basic ingredients of science fiction, was put to hilarious use in *Back to the Future* (1985). Beginning in the present, the film introduces a personable young man named Marty McFly (the personable Michael J. Fox), who becomes involved with a crazy scientist (Christopher Lloyd) who invents a time machine that shoots Marty back to 1955 where he meets the girl who will become his mother. She (Lea Thompson) becomes smitten with him, which Marty realizes is a big problem — because unless she falls in love with and marries the man (Crispen Glover) who will become his father, there will never be a Marty. Things take a chaotic course when his time machine breaks down, thereby possibly dumping him permanently in 1955. This results in a frantic search to locate his scientist friend. Eventually, the harried Marty gets back to the present, having successfully played matchmaker to his parents-to-be; but the present now seems a lot sweeter to him than it used to be. *Back to the Future* is a joy of a trip.

Back to the Future, Part Two (1989): Michael J. Fox, Christopher Lloyd, and Dog.

Neil Simon's *Brighton Beach Memoirs* with Jonathan Silverman as Eugene.

The enormous success that Neil Simon has enjoyed in the theater is reflected to almost the same degree with the filmed versions of his comedy creations. That success moved onto a more personal plane with a series of plays based upon his own life as a youngster in Brooklyn.

First came *Brighton Beach Memoirs* (1986), starring Jonathan Silverman as Eugene, a teenager emerging from puberty and locked in constant conflict with his parents, brother, and relatives sharing the same house. Director Gene Saks, the Simon director par excellence, captured the late thirties as his setting along with the warmth, humor, anguish, and confusion that make up the life of young Eugene.

Anguish and confusion of another kind come to Eugene when he joins the Army, a litany of comedy and travail crafted by Neil Simon in his *Biloxi Blues* (1988). This time, the earnest, fumbling, and largely innocent Eugene is played by Matthew Broderick, who neatly conveys the discomforts of a lad moving from a mother's love in Brooklyn to the cold-hearted commands of a slightly psychotic sergeant (Christopher Walken) in a Mississippi boot camp. Inevitably, he makes his sexual breakthrough in the arms of a benevolent Dixie lady-for-hire. *Brighton Beach Memoirs* and *Biloxi Blues* — pure Simon.

More Simon: *Biloxi Blues*, this time with Matthew Broderick as Eugene, sharing company with Penelope Ann Miller.

Dragnet: Dan Aykroyd as Sergeant Friday and Tom Hanks as Streebek—plainclothes cops except on occasion.

Dragnet (1987) brought together two of the strongest shows in television history: the greatly successful series of the same name that started in 1952, and one of the greatest comedy shows, *Saturday Night Live,* with one of its graduates — Dan Aykroyd. The film gently parodies the old series with Aykroyd as Joe Friday, nephew of Jack Webb. The nephew is every bit as serious, humorless, and monosyllabic ("Just the facts, Ma'am") as his uncle as he operates in a Los Angeles described as "the capital of depravity in what passes as the modern world." His chief adversaries are a publisher of porno magazines (Dabney Coleman), a crooked minister (Christopher Plummer) involved with missing toxic chemicals, and a band of drug-crazed PAGANS (People Against Goodness and Normalcy). Crime stands no chance against the rigidly square Friday as he cruises around dressed in his 1950's hat and suit.

Dragnet is a triumph for Aykroyd, who comes uncannily close to the diction and style of Jack Webb. The film was also another step forward for Tom Hanks, playing Friday's flippant partner, constantly puzzled by the old-fashioned style and language of the man with whom he must ride around fighting crime. With talents like Aykroyd and Hanks, film comedy has as promising a future as it has a solid past.

Midnight Run (1988) might well have been titled *The Odd Couple on the Run.* The pairing of Robert De Niro as an ex-Chicago cop turned bounty hunter and Charles Grodin as an embezzling accountant is about as odd a couple as have ever spent time together. The bounty hunter is tough, cynical, and hyperactive; the accountant is quiet, low-key, and philosophical. The job of the one man is to get the other from New York to Los Angeles in order to pick up a $100,000 fee from the people who have put up the accountant's bail. The problem is that other people also want the accountant, including the FBI, the Mafia chieftain whom the accountant has swindled, and a rival bounty hunter — all of whom make the trek across the country a whirlwind of car chases, gun fights, and brawls. Through it all, the accountant gently chides the distraught bounty man about his bad personal habits, smoking, eating junk food, and lifestyle in general. In the end, it is the accountant himself who rewards his harried escort — before disappearing into the night.

Midnight Run is like a Hope-Crosby road picture set in the horror of the underworld and somehow managing to combine violent and raunchy humor with charm. That it does so is due entirely to the talents of De Niro and Grodin.

Midnight Run: John Ashton, Charles Grodin, and Robert De Niro.

. . . and to end on a happy note, *Field of Dreams* (1989), a beautiful fantasy about a man (Kevin Costner) who builds a baseball field on his farm in order to meet his baseball-playing father as a young man. *Field of Dreams* proves that there will always be an audience for films that deal kindly with the human spirit.

INDEX

The Best of Universal
by Tony Thomas
was composed in 10 on 12 Souvenir Light on a
Compugraphic 9600 G with display
type in Souvenir Bold
by Thunder Projects Inc., Vestal, NY;
printed by sheet-fed offset on 70-pound acid-free
Sterling Litho Satin;
bound in 12-point coated stock
by Johnson City Printing, Binghamton, NY ;
and published by the Vestal Press, Ltd.
Vestal, NY 13851-0097

Cover design by Grace L. Houghton

Tony Thomas has written over thirty film books and is eminently qualified to give an overview of the best films of Universal. His long association with the Hollywood community as a respected author, TV producer, narrator, and freelance writer give him the perspective and background to select which films were milestones, which endured as classics, and which were memorable.

Some of Mr. Thomas' books have focused on the lives and films of some of Hollywood's best-known film personalities: Errol Flynn, Busby Berkeley, Peter Ustinov, Kirk Douglas, Sam Wood, Gene Kelly, Harry Warren, Burt Lancaster, Marlon Brando, Gregory Peck, Ronald Reagan, Olivia de Havilland, Henry Fonda, George Sanders, James Stewart, Howard Hughes, and Joel McCrea. Topics have ranged from film music, musicals, and dance to adventure.

Mr. Thomas began his career as an announcer with the Canadian Broadcasting Corporation in 1948. In 1957 he was appointed a radio producer and for two years produced the nightly network show *Assignment,* then went to the CBC Special Programs division. His first trip to Hollywood was in 1959 to collect material for radio and TV programs about the film industry. Since then, Mr. Thomas has specialized in that area.

Since his move to Los Angeles in 1967, he has continued to provide material for CBC, has appeared for several years as a panelist on *Flashback,* and has served as host and writer of a one-year variety series, *As Time Goes By.* His more recent books include *The Films of 20th Century Fox, Film Score,* and *Notes on Adventure.* He wrote the ABC Special, *The 50 Years of Warner Brothers* (1973), was writer-producer of the ABC-20th Century Fox television series *That's Hollywood* (1977–81), and more recently narrated the CBS Specials *The Kennedy Center Honors* and narrated *The AFI Salute to . . .* (since 1978). He has been writer for the PBS *Meeting of the Minds,* the 1979 and 1984 *Academy Award Show,* writer for *The American Movie Awards* (NBC), narrator for *The Golden Globe Awards,* producer-writer-host for *Back to the Stage Door Canteen* (PBS), *The West that Never Was* (PBS and BBC), *Coming Next Week . . . Long Ago,* and *Film Score: The Music of the Movies.*

He is currently involved in producing documentaries in the U.S., the U.K., and in Europe.

LaVergne, TN USA
01 December 2010
206911LV00001B/30/P